FUN FACTS BOOK

FOR KIDS 8-12

1,699 Interesting Random Facts
For Smart Kids & Curious Minds

ISBN: 978-1-948652-85-8

Published by: Bella Mente Press Cover design and layout © 2026 Bella Mente Press.
Printed in the United States of America

TABLE OF CONTENTS

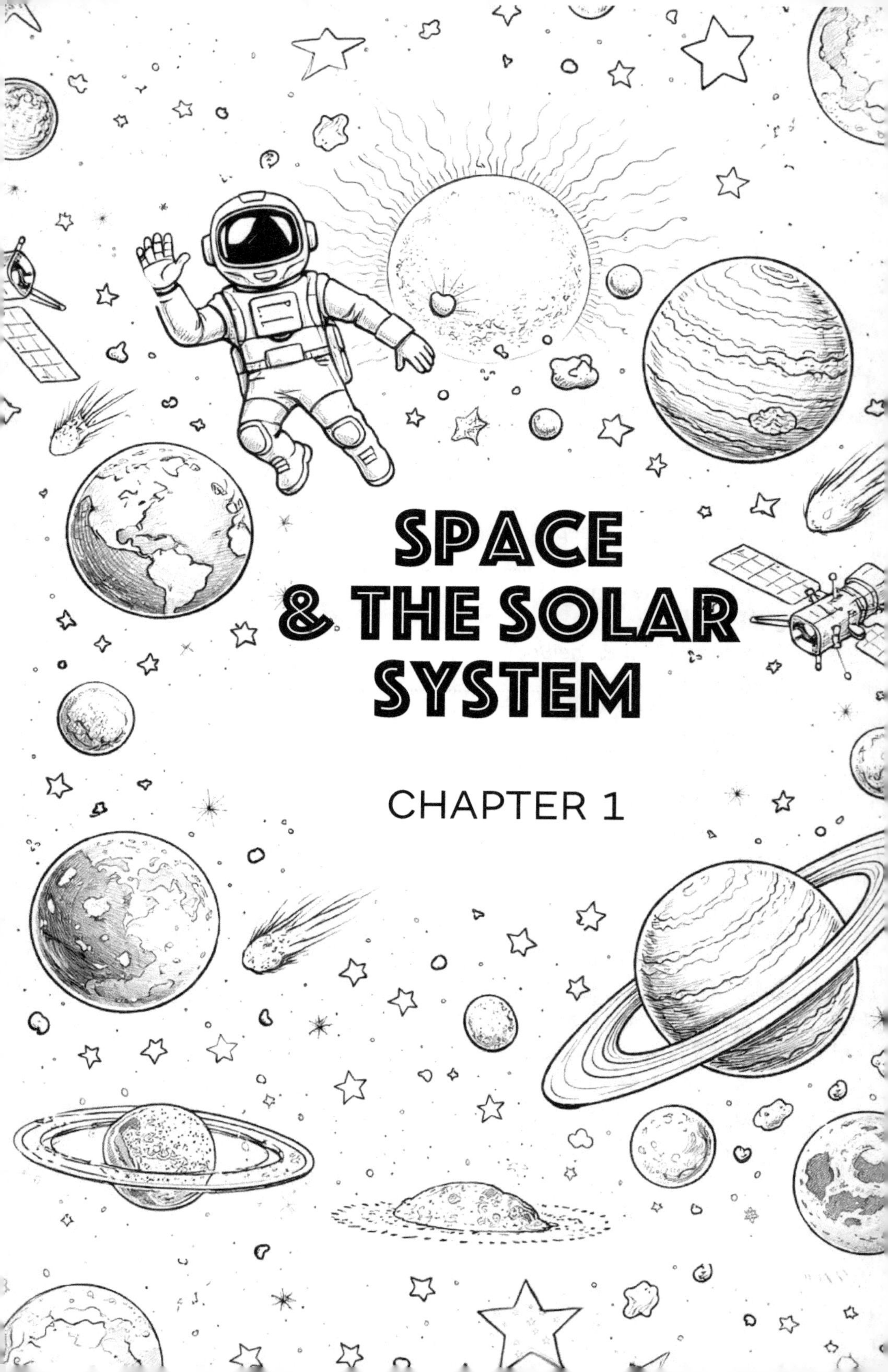

SPACE & THE SOLAR SYSTEM

CHAPTER 1

1 THERE ARE MORE STARS IN THE UNIVERSE THAN GRAINS OF SAND ON ALL THE BEACHES ON EARTH.

2 A SINGLE TEASPOON OF A NEUTRON STAR WOULD WEIGH ABOUT 6 BILLION TONS.

3 IF YOU COULD DRIVE YOUR CAR STRAIGHT UP AT HIGHWAY SPEEDS, YOU WOULD ARRIVE IN SPACE IN JUST OVER AN HOUR.

4 ASTRONAUTS SAY THE MOON SMELLS LIKE GUNPOWDER.

5 MORE THAN ONE MILLION EARTHS COULD FIT INSIDE THE SUN.

6 "JINGLE BELLS" WAS THE FIRST SONG PLAYED IN SPACE.

7 COCA-COLA WAS THE FIRST SOFT DRINK CONSUMED IN SPACE.

8 NASA ASTRONAUTS HAVE A PATCH OF VELCRO SEWN INTO THEIR HELMETS SO THAT THEY CAN SCRATCH THEIR NOSES.

9 GOLD IS CREATED WHEN NEUTRON STARS COLLIDE, AND A COLLISION CAN PRODUCE ENOUGH GOLD TO FILL 200 EARTHS.

10 THE MOON IS A QUARTER OF THE SIZE OF EARTH.

11 THE EARTH'S CORE IS HOTTER THAN THE SURFACE OF THE SUN.

12 EARTH IS THE ONLY PLANET IN THE SOLAR SYSTEM THAT HAS ENOUGH OXYGEN FOR FIRE TO BURN.

13 OUTER SPACE IS COMPLETELY SILENT DUE TO THE LACK OF AIR TO CARRY SOUND WAVES.

14 SATURN CHANGES COLOR WITH THE SEASONS, LOOKING BLUE IN THE WINTER AND YELLOW IN THE SUMMER.

15 IT TAKES 8 MINUTES AND 20 SECONDS FOR LIGHT FROM THE SUN TO REACH EARTH.

16 ASTRONAUTS' BONES BECOME WEAKER THE LONGER THEY STAY IN SPACE.

17 JUST AS EARTH EXPERIENCES EARTHQUAKES, THE MOON EXPERIENCES MOONQUAKES.

18 ASTRONAUTS GET ABOUT 3%, OR UP TO TWO INCHES, TALLER IN SPACE BECAUSE THERE IS NO GRAVITY PUSHING DOWN ON THEIR SPINES.

19 THE HEAT FROM THE BIG BANG STILL WARMS PARTS OF THE UNIVERSE TODAY.

20 THE FIRST FOOD GROWN IN SPACE WAS POTATOES.

21 ON SATURN, EACH SEASON LASTS ABOUT SEVEN EARTH YEARS.

22 SUNSETS ON MARS APPEAR BLUE.

23 95% PERCENT OF THE UNIVERSE IS CONSIDERED INVISIBLE.

24 THE SUN APPEARS WHITE WHEN VIEWED FROM SPACE.

25 THE SUN IS ALMOST PERFECTLY ROUND, UNLIKE EARTH.

26 JUPITER IS MORE THAN TWICE THE SIZE OF ALL THE OTHER PLANETS IN THE SOLAR SYSTEM COMBINED.

27 VENUS TAKES 243 EARTH DAYS TO ROTATE ONCE BUT ONLY 225 EARTH DAYS TO ORBIT THE SUN, MAKING A SINGLE DAY ON VENUS LONGER THAN A YEAR.

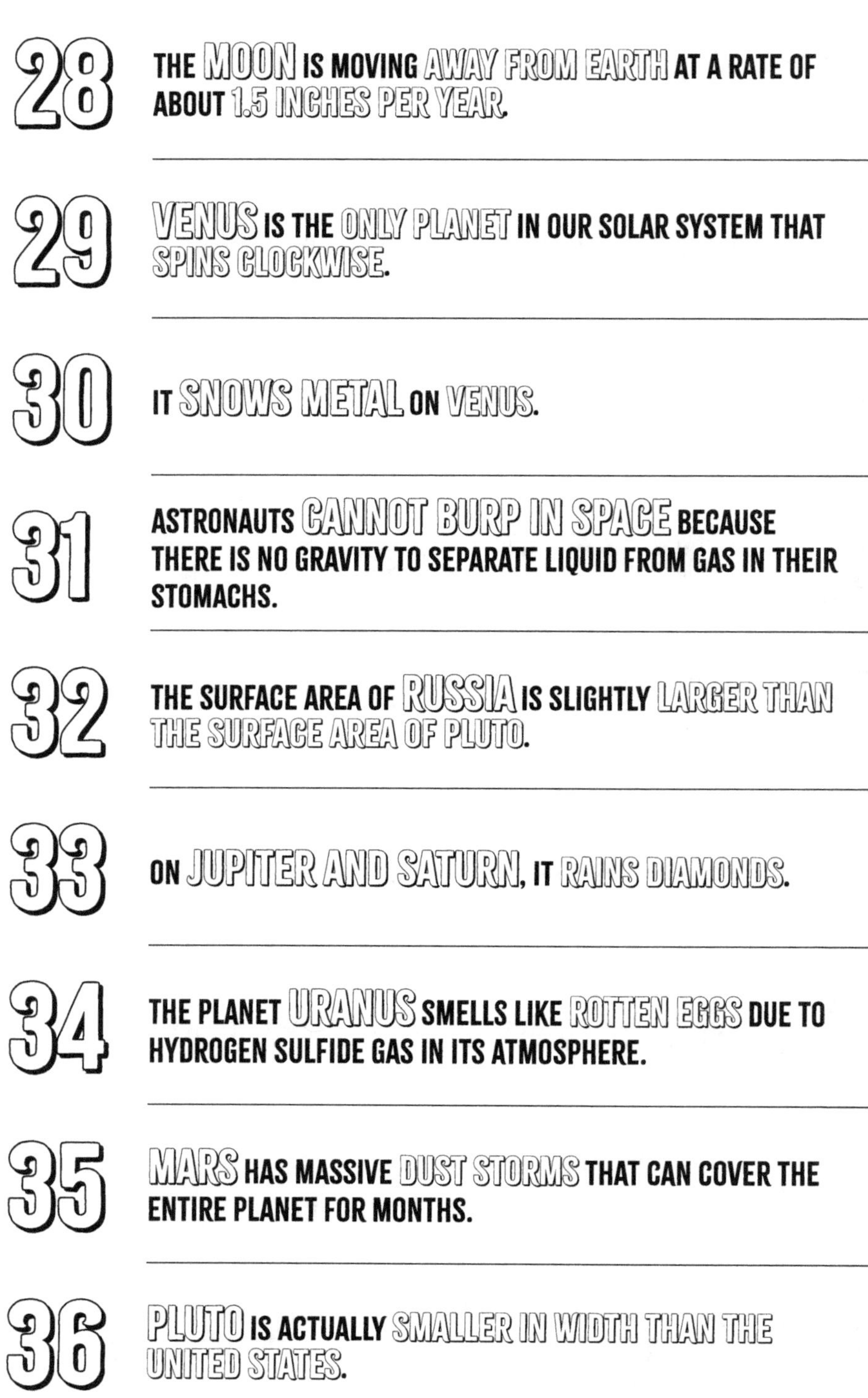

28 THE MOON IS MOVING AWAY FROM EARTH AT A RATE OF ABOUT 1.5 INCHES PER YEAR.

---

29 VENUS IS THE ONLY PLANET IN OUR SOLAR SYSTEM THAT SPINS CLOCKWISE.

---

30 IT SNOWS METAL ON VENUS.

---

31 ASTRONAUTS CANNOT BURP IN SPACE BECAUSE THERE IS NO GRAVITY TO SEPARATE LIQUID FROM GAS IN THEIR STOMACHS.

---

32 THE SURFACE AREA OF RUSSIA IS SLIGHTLY LARGER THAN THE SURFACE AREA OF PLUTO.

---

33 ON JUPITER AND SATURN, IT RAINS DIAMONDS.

---

34 THE PLANET URANUS SMELLS LIKE ROTTEN EGGS DUE TO HYDROGEN SULFIDE GAS IN ITS ATMOSPHERE.

---

35 MARS HAS MASSIVE DUST STORMS THAT CAN COVER THE ENTIRE PLANET FOR MONTHS.

---

36 PLUTO IS ACTUALLY SMALLER IN WIDTH THAN THE UNITED STATES.

A FULL NASA SPACE SUIT COSTS ABOUT $12 MILLION.

FOOTPRINTS LEFT BY ASTRONAUTS ON THE MOON WILL STAY THERE FOR MILLIONS OF YEARS BECAUSE THERE IS NO WIND TO BLOW THEM AWAY.

THE INTERNATIONAL SPACE STATION CIRCLES EARTH ONCE EVERY 90 MINUTES.

SCIENTISTS DISCOVERED A PLANET CALLED 55 CANCRI E THAT IS MADE LARGELY OF DIAMOND.

JUPITER SPINS SO FAST THAT A DAY THERE LASTS LESS THAN 10 HOURS.

SATURN IS THE ONLY PLANET THAT IS LESS DENSE THAN WATER, MEANING IT WOULD FLOAT IN A GIANT BATHTUB.

PIZZA HUT ONCE DELIVERED A PIZZA TO ASTRONAUTS ON THE INTERNATIONAL SPACE STATION.

VENUS IS THE HOTTEST PLANET IN THE SOLAR SYSTEM, EVEN THOUGH MERCURY IS CLOSER TO THE SUN.

SATURN'S RINGS ARE MOSTLY MADE OF CHUNKS OF ICE AND ROCK.

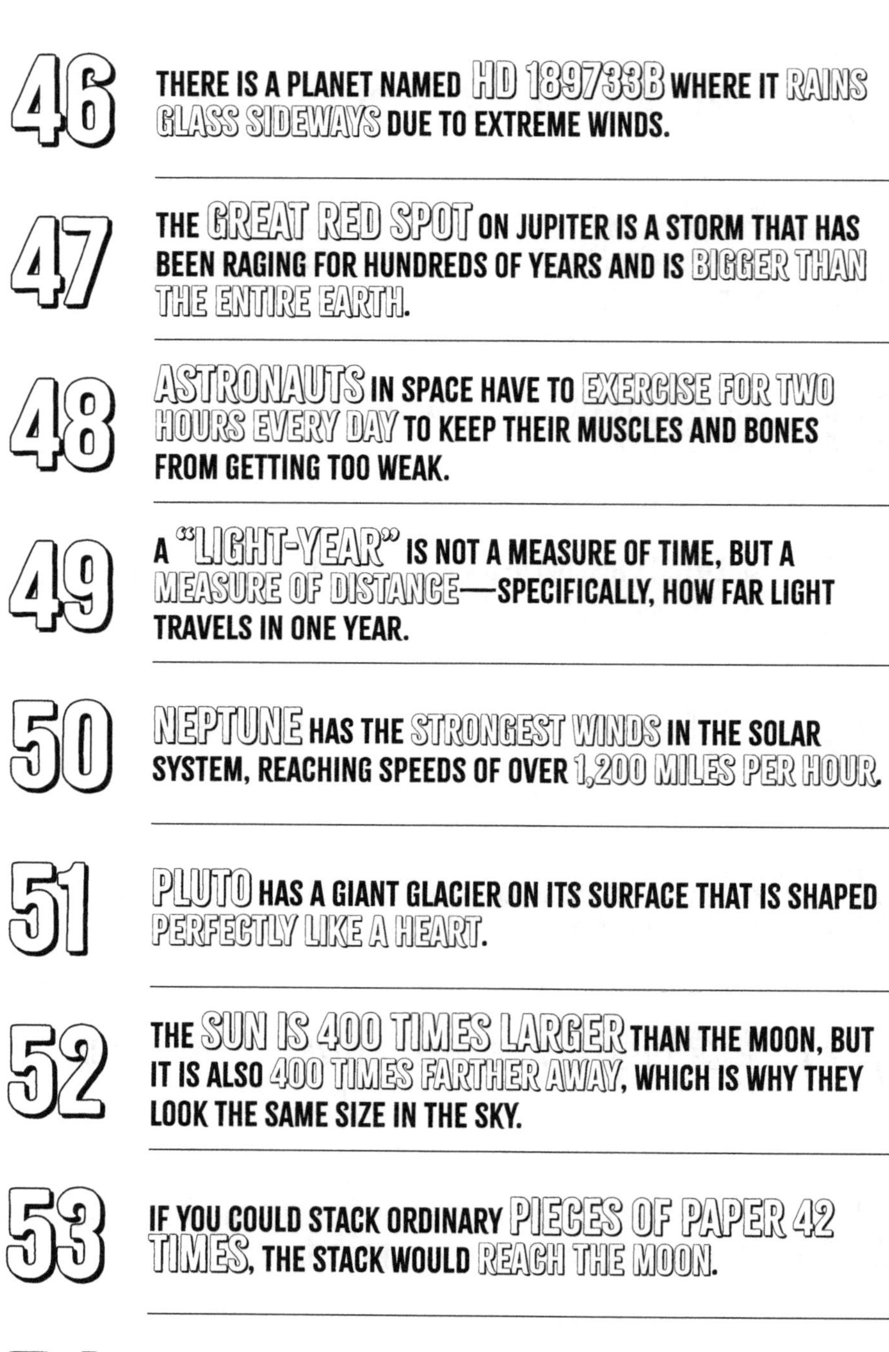

46 THERE IS A PLANET NAMED HD 189733B WHERE IT RAINS GLASS SIDEWAYS DUE TO EXTREME WINDS.

47 THE GREAT RED SPOT ON JUPITER IS A STORM THAT HAS BEEN RAGING FOR HUNDREDS OF YEARS AND IS BIGGER THAN THE ENTIRE EARTH.

48 ASTRONAUTS IN SPACE HAVE TO EXERCISE FOR TWO HOURS EVERY DAY TO KEEP THEIR MUSCLES AND BONES FROM GETTING TOO WEAK.

49 A "LIGHT-YEAR" IS NOT A MEASURE OF TIME, BUT A MEASURE OF DISTANCE—SPECIFICALLY, HOW FAR LIGHT TRAVELS IN ONE YEAR.

50 NEPTUNE HAS THE STRONGEST WINDS IN THE SOLAR SYSTEM, REACHING SPEEDS OF OVER 1,200 MILES PER HOUR.

51 PLUTO HAS A GIANT GLACIER ON ITS SURFACE THAT IS SHAPED PERFECTLY LIKE A HEART.

52 THE SUN IS 400 TIMES LARGER THAN THE MOON, BUT IT IS ALSO 400 TIMES FARTHER AWAY, WHICH IS WHY THEY LOOK THE SAME SIZE IN THE SKY.

53 IF YOU COULD STACK ORDINARY PIECES OF PAPER 42 TIMES, THE STACK WOULD REACH THE MOON.

54 THE MOON IS NOT ROUND LIKE A BALL; IT IS SHAPED MORE LIKE A LEMON.

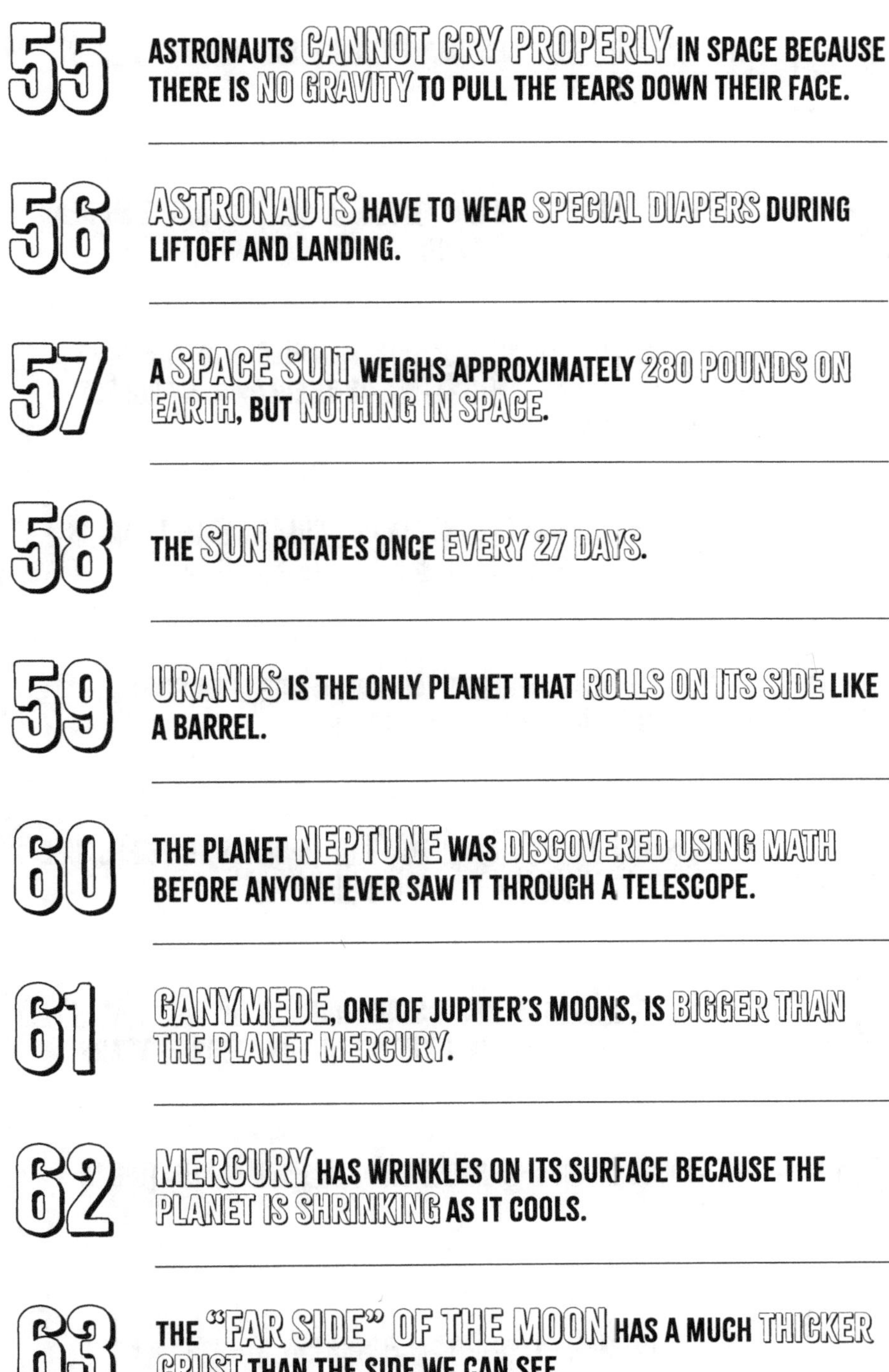

55 ASTRONAUTS CANNOT CRY PROPERLY IN SPACE BECAUSE THERE IS NO GRAVITY TO PULL THE TEARS DOWN THEIR FACE.

56 ASTRONAUTS HAVE TO WEAR SPECIAL DIAPERS DURING LIFTOFF AND LANDING.

57 A SPACE SUIT WEIGHS APPROXIMATELY 280 POUNDS ON EARTH, BUT NOTHING IN SPACE.

58 THE SUN ROTATES ONCE EVERY 27 DAYS.

59 URANUS IS THE ONLY PLANET THAT ROLLS ON ITS SIDE LIKE A BARREL.

60 THE PLANET NEPTUNE WAS DISCOVERED USING MATH BEFORE ANYONE EVER SAW IT THROUGH A TELESCOPE.

61 GANYMEDE, ONE OF JUPITER'S MOONS, IS BIGGER THAN THE PLANET MERCURY.

62 MERCURY HAS WRINKLES ON ITS SURFACE BECAUSE THE PLANET IS SHRINKING AS IT COOLS.

63 THE "FAR SIDE" OF THE MOON HAS A MUCH THICKER CRUST THAN THE SIDE WE CAN SEE.

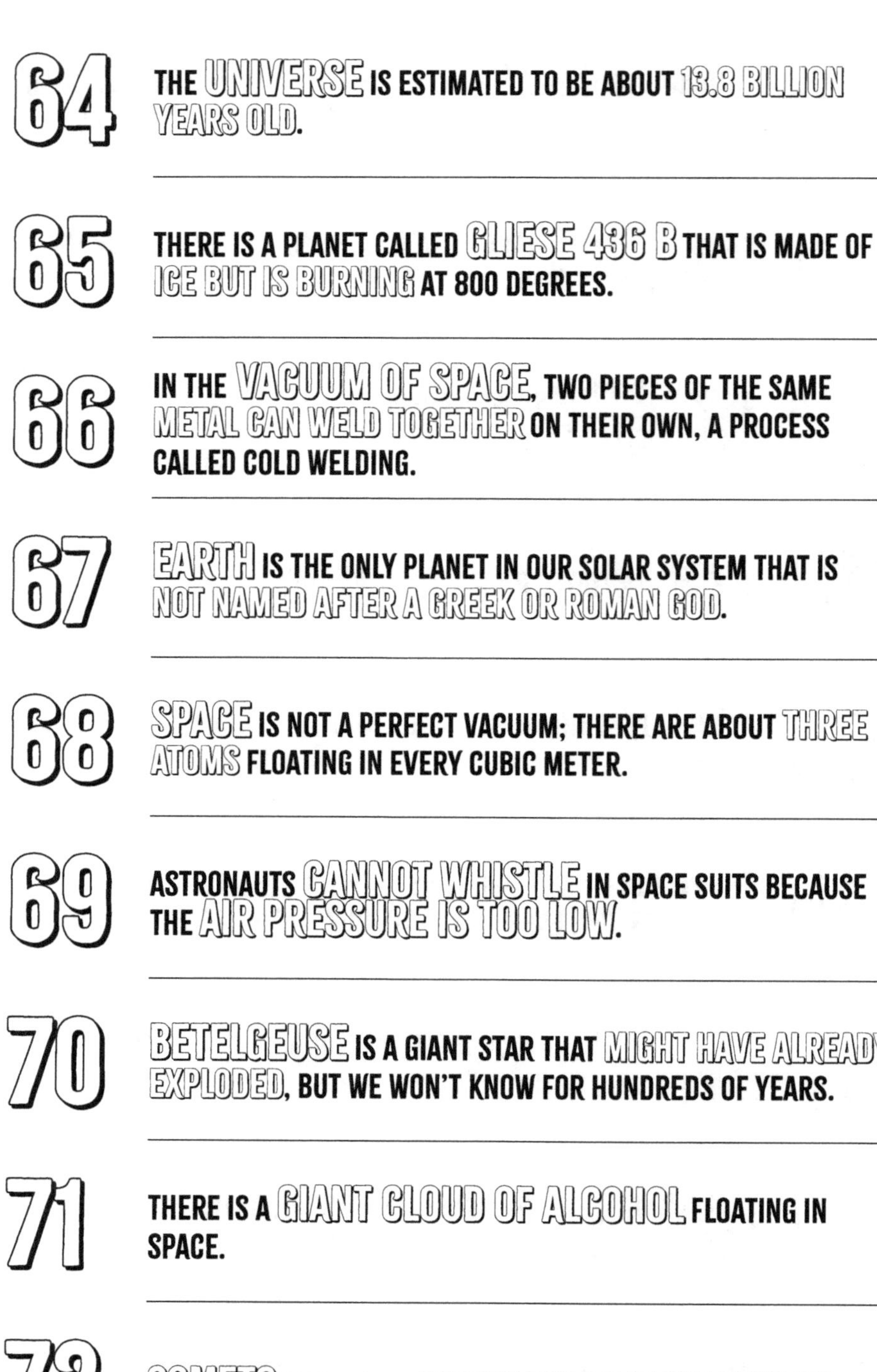

64 THE UNIVERSE IS ESTIMATED TO BE ABOUT 13.8 BILLION YEARS OLD.

---

65 THERE IS A PLANET CALLED GLIESE 436 B THAT IS MADE OF ICE BUT IS BURNING AT 800 DEGREES.

---

66 IN THE VACUUM OF SPACE, TWO PIECES OF THE SAME METAL CAN WELD TOGETHER ON THEIR OWN, A PROCESS CALLED COLD WELDING.

---

67 EARTH IS THE ONLY PLANET IN OUR SOLAR SYSTEM THAT IS NOT NAMED AFTER A GREEK OR ROMAN GOD.

---

68 SPACE IS NOT A PERFECT VACUUM; THERE ARE ABOUT THREE ATOMS FLOATING IN EVERY CUBIC METER.

---

69 ASTRONAUTS CANNOT WHISTLE IN SPACE SUITS BECAUSE THE AIR PRESSURE IS TOO LOW.

---

70 BETELGEUSE IS A GIANT STAR THAT MIGHT HAVE ALREADY EXPLODED, BUT WE WON'T KNOW FOR HUNDREDS OF YEARS.

---

71 THERE IS A GIANT CLOUD OF ALCOHOL FLOATING IN SPACE.

---

72 COMETS SMELL LIKE ROTTEN EGGS AND KITTY LITTER.

73 YOU CAN SEE THE BORDER BETWEEN EAST AND WEST BERLIN FROM SPACE AT NIGHT BECAUSE OF THE DIFFERENT LIGHTBULBS.

---

74 FREEZE-DRIED FOOD WAS POPULARIZED BY SPACE MISSIONS.

---

75 THE APOLLO 11 ASTRONAUTS HAD TO GO THROUGH CUSTOMS WHEN THEY RETURNED FROM THE MOON.

---

76 THE SUN ACCOUNTS FOR 99.8% OF THE MASS OF THE ENTIRE SOLAR SYSTEM.

---

77 IF YOU WEIGH 100 POUNDS ON EARTH, YOU WOULD WEIGH ONLY 38 POUNDS ON MARS.

---

78 ASTRONAUTS ON THE INTERNATIONAL SPACE STATION SEE 16 SUNRISES AND SUNSETS EVERY SINGLE DAY.

---

79 THE AMERICAN FLAG LEFT ON THE MOON HAS LIKELY BEEN BLEACHED COMPLETELY WHITE BY THE SUN'S RADIATION.

---

80 ASTRONAUT CHARLES DUKE LEFT A FAMILY PHOTO ON THE SURFACE OF THE MOON IN 1972, AND IT IS STILL THERE.

---

81 MARS HAS THE TALLEST MOUNTAIN IN THE SOLAR SYSTEM, OLYMPUS MONS, WHICH IS THREE TIMES TALLER THAN MOUNT EVEREST.

82 LIGHT TRAVELS AT A SPEED OF 186,000 MILES PER SECOND.

83 AN ASTRONAUT'S HEART ACTUALLY GETS ROUNDER WHEN THEY ARE IN SPACE.

84 SATURN HAS A GIANT STORM AT ITS NORTH POLE THAT IS SHAPED LIKE A PERFECT HEXAGON.

85 TARDIGRADES (WATER BEARS) CAN SURVIVE IN OUTER SPACE AND EXTREME RADIATION.

86 THE INTERNATIONAL SPACE STATION IS THE MOST EXPENSIVE OBJECT EVER BUILT BY HUMANS (ABOUT $150 BILLION).

87 THERE IS A "GRAVEYARD ORBIT" IN SPACE WHERE OLD SATELLITES ARE PUSHED SO THEY DON'T CRASH INTO ACTIVE ONES.

88 THE "DARK SIDE" OF THE MOON ACTUALLY GETS JUST AS MUCH SUNLIGHT AS THE FRONT; WE JUST NEVER SEE IT.

89 SCIENTISTS BELIEVE THE CENTER OF THE MILKY WAY GALAXY SMELLS LIKE RUM AND TASTES LIKE RASPBERRIES DUE TO THE CHEMICALS THERE.

90 JUPITER HAS 95 CONFIRMED MOONS.

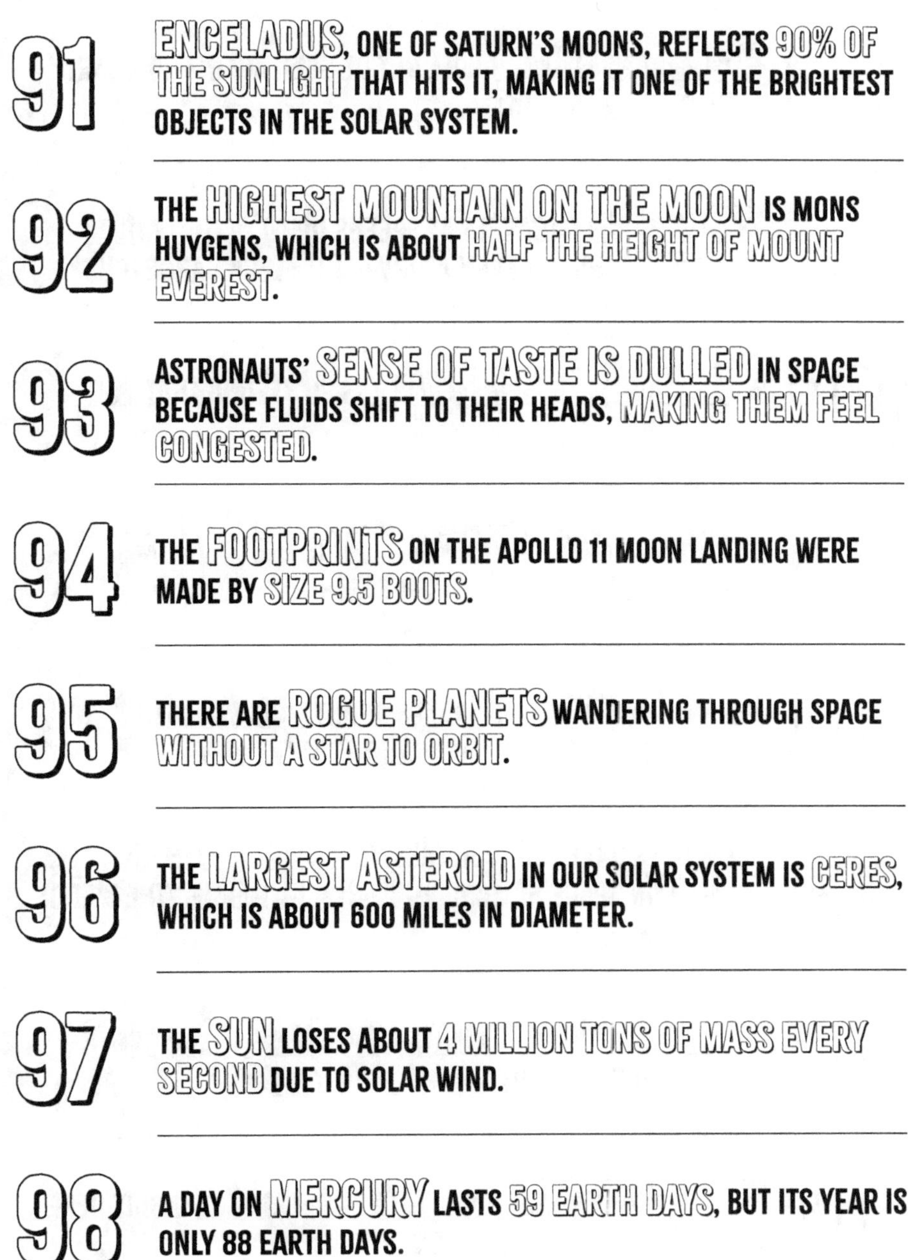

91 ENCELADUS, ONE OF SATURN'S MOONS, REFLECTS 90% OF THE SUNLIGHT THAT HITS IT, MAKING IT ONE OF THE BRIGHTEST OBJECTS IN THE SOLAR SYSTEM.

---

92 THE HIGHEST MOUNTAIN ON THE MOON IS MONS HUYGENS, WHICH IS ABOUT HALF THE HEIGHT OF MOUNT EVEREST.

---

93 ASTRONAUTS' SENSE OF TASTE IS DULLED IN SPACE BECAUSE FLUIDS SHIFT TO THEIR HEADS, MAKING THEM FEEL CONGESTED.

---

94 THE FOOTPRINTS ON THE APOLLO 11 MOON LANDING WERE MADE BY SIZE 9.5 BOOTS.

---

95 THERE ARE ROGUE PLANETS WANDERING THROUGH SPACE WITHOUT A STAR TO ORBIT.

---

96 THE LARGEST ASTEROID IN OUR SOLAR SYSTEM IS CERES, WHICH IS ABOUT 600 MILES IN DIAMETER.

---

97 THE SUN LOSES ABOUT 4 MILLION TONS OF MASS EVERY SECOND DUE TO SOLAR WIND.

---

98 A DAY ON MERCURY LASTS 59 EARTH DAYS, BUT ITS YEAR IS ONLY 88 EARTH DAYS.

---

99 THE MILKY WAY GALAXY IS HURTLING THROUGH SPACE AT ABOUT 1.3 MILLION MILES PER HOUR.

100 HALLEY'S COMET WILL NOT BE SEEN AGAIN FROM EARTH UNTIL THE YEAR 2061.

---

101 SPACE JUNK TRAVELS AT SPEEDS UP TO 17,500 MILES PER HOUR, MAKING EVEN A TINY PAINT FLECK DANGEROUS.

---

102 A BLACK HOLE'S GRAVITY IS SO STRONG THAT NOT EVEN LIGHT CAN ESCAPE IT.

---

103 THE VOYAGER 1 SPACECRAFT IS THE FARTHEST HUMAN-MADE OBJECT FROM EARTH.

---

104 THE SOLAR SYSTEM TAKES ABOUT 230 MILLION YEARS TO COMPLETE ONE ORBIT AROUND THE MILKY WAY.

---

105 SCIENTISTS HAVE FOUND A MASSIVE WATER VAPOR CLOUD IN SPACE HOLDING 140 TRILLION TIMES THE WATER IN EARTH'S OCEANS.

---

106 THE MILKY WAY AND ANDROMEDA GALAXIES WILL COLLIDE IN ABOUT 4.5 BILLION YEARS.

---

107 MERCURY HAS ANCIENT WATER ICE HIDDEN INSIDE DEEP, PERMANENTLY SHADOWED CRATERS.

---

108 BLACK HOLES CAN STRETCH OBJECTS OUT LIKE A NOODLE IN A PROCESS CALLED "SPAGHETTIFICATION".

109 JUPITER'S MOON IO HAS ACTIVE VOLCANOES THAT SHOOT LAVA 250 MILES INTO THE AIR.

---

110 THERE IS AN EXOPLANET CALLED WASP-76B WHERE THE WEATHER IS SO HOT THAT IT RAINS LIQUID IRON.

---

111 SATURN'S MOON TITAN HAS LAKES AND RIVERS FILLED WITH LIQUID METHANE INSTEAD OF WATER.

---

112 JUMPING OFF THE HIGHEST CLIFF IN THE SOLAR SYSTEM, LOCATED ON URANUS'S MOON MIRANDA, WOULD TAKE 12 MINUTES BEFORE HITTING THE BOTTOM.

---

113 SEEDS TAKEN TO ORBIT THE MOON DURING THE APOLLO 14 MISSION WERE LATER PLANTED ON EARTH AND GREW INTO NORMAL "MOON TREES".

---

114 ASTRONOMERS HAVE COUNTED OVER 1,600 MAJOR VOLCANOES ON VENUS, THE MOST OF ANY PLANET.

---

115 THE LARGEST KNOWN STAR, UY SCUTI, IS SO HUGE IT WOULD SWALLOW JUPITER IF IT REPLACED OUR SUN.

---

116 THE MOON IS "TIDALLY LOCKED" TO EARTH, MEANING WE ONLY EVER GET TO SEE ONE SIDE OF IT.

---

117 THE BOÖTES VOID IS A MASSIVE, SPHERICAL REGION OF SPACE THAT IS BIZARRELY EMPTY OF GALAXIES.

118 THE SUN GENERATES DEEP ACOUSTIC WAVES THAT BOUNCE AROUND ITS INTERIOR, ESSENTIALLY MAKING IT "SING".

119 NEWLY BORN NEUTRON STARS CAN SPIN UP TO 600 TIMES A SECOND.

120 BECAUSE URANUS ORBITS ON ITS SIDE, ITS RINGS AND MOONS ORBIT TOP-TO-BOTTOM RATHER THAN LEFT-TO-RIGHT.

121 IN 2017, A FAST-MOVING SPACE ROCK NAMED ‘OUMUAMUA BECAME THE FIRST KNOWN OBJECT FROM ANOTHER STAR SYSTEM TO VISIT OURS.

122 THE BACKGROUND TEMPERATURE OF DEEP SPACE IS ABOUT MINUS 455 DEGREES FAHRENHEIT.

123 THE LARGEST AND OLDEST KNOWN IMPACT CRATER IN THE SOLAR SYSTEM IS LOCATED ON THE SOUTH POLE OF OUR MOON.

124 A SINGLE DAY ON PLUTO TAKES ABOUT 153 HOURS TO COMPLETE.

125 A SMALL ROGUE STAR PASSED THROUGH THE OUTER EDGES OF OUR SOLAR SYSTEM 70,000 YEARS AGO.

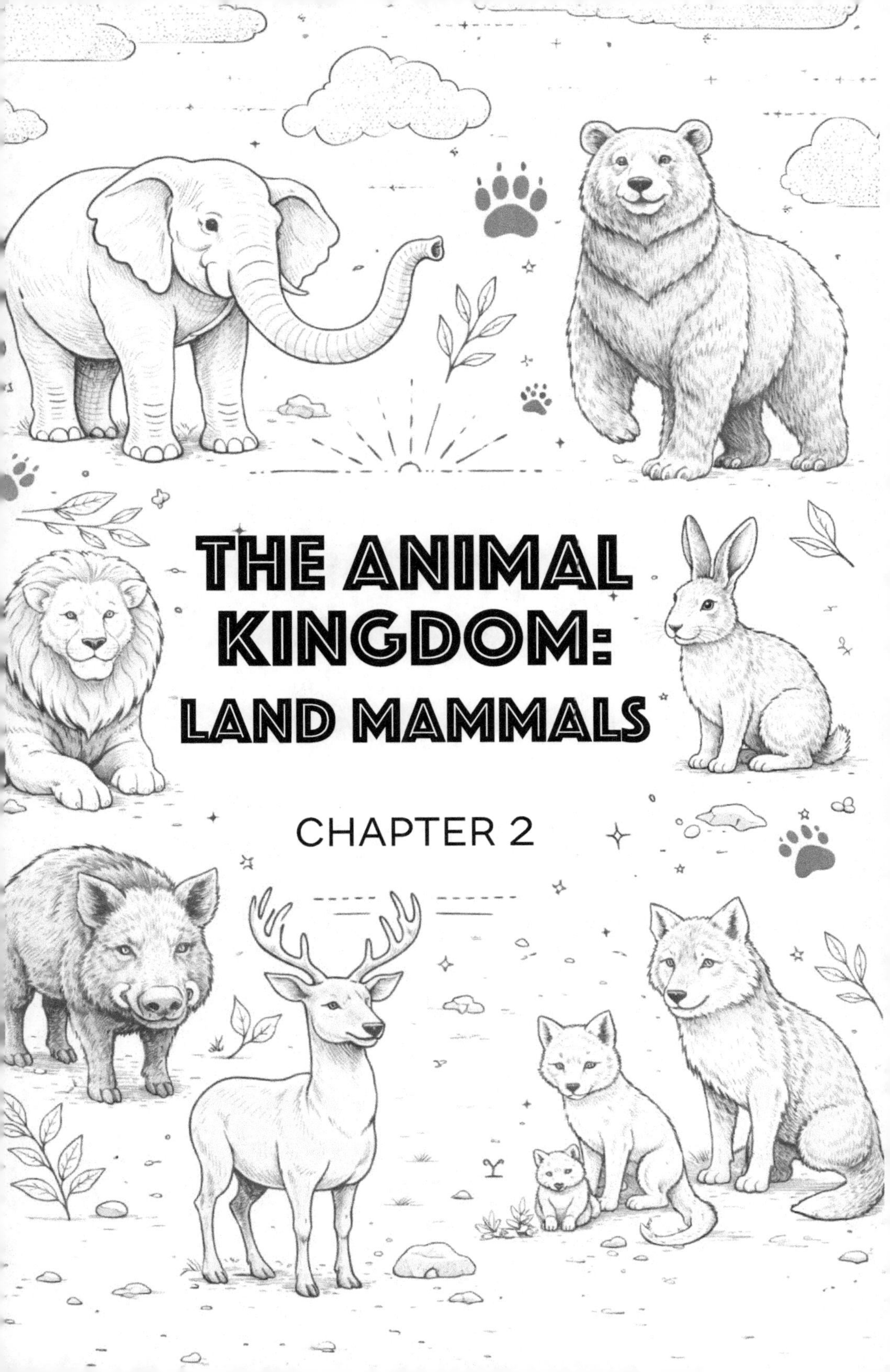

THE ANIMAL KINGDOM: LAND MAMMALS

CHAPTER 2

126 TIGERS HAVE STRIPED SKIN, NOT JUST STRIPED FUR.

127 TIGERS HAVE WHITE SPOTS ON THE BACKS OF THEIR EARS THAT LOOK LIKE EYES TO SCARE OFF PREDATORS ATTACKING FROM BEHIND.

128 TIGER SALIVA IS ANTISEPTIC AND CAN HELP HEAL THEIR WOUNDS.

129 A CHEETAH CAN SPEED UP FASTER THAN A RACE CAR.

130 THE CHEETAH IS THE ONLY BIG CAT THAT CANNOT ROAR.

131 LIONS ARE THE ONLY BIG CATS THAT LIVE IN SOCIAL GROUPS.

132 MALE LIONS SLEEP FOR ABOUT 20 HOURS A DAY.

133 A LION'S ROAR CAN BE HEARD FROM UP TO FIVE MILES AWAY.

134 JAGUARS' EYES ARE MORE POWERFUL AT NIGHT THAN DURING THE DAY, HELPING THEM TO HUNT IN THE DARK.

135 A JAGUAR HAS THE STRONGEST BITE OF ALL BIG CATS AND CAN BITE THROUGH A TURTLE SHELL.

---

136 SNOW LEOPARDS KEEP WARM BY WRAPPING THEIR LONG, FLUFFY TAIL AROUND THEIR BODIES.

---

137 SNOW LEOPARDS CANNOT ROAR; THEY PURR AND MEOW LIKE HOUSE CATS.

---

138 A "BLACK PANTHER" IS NOT A SPECIFIC SPECIES; IT IS JUST A JAGUAR OR LEOPARD WITH BLACK FUR.

---

139 HYENAS ARE NOT ACTUALLY DOGS; THEY ARE MORE CLOSELY RELATED TO CATS.

---

140 HYENAS "LAUGH" WHEN THEY ARE STRESSED OR EXCITED, NOT WHEN THEY ARE HAPPY.

---

141 A GRIZZLY BEAR CAN RUN AS FAST AS A HORSE.

---

142 A GRIZZLY BEAR'S BITE IS STRONG ENOUGH TO CRUSH A BOWLING BALL.

---

143 POLAR BEARS HAVE BLACK SKIN UNDER THEIR WHITE FUR TO HELP ABSORB HEAT FROM THE SUN.

144 POLAR BEARS HAVE BEEN KNOWN TO SWIM FOR 60 MILES WITHOUT RESTING.

---

145 ELEPHANTS ARE NOT ABLE TO JUMP.

---

146 BABY ELEPHANTS SUCK THEIR TRUNKS FOR COMFORT, JUST LIKE HUMAN BABIES SUCK THEIR THUMBS.

---

147 ELEPHANTS ARE ONE OF THE FEW ANIMALS THAT CAN RECOGNIZE THEMSELVES IN A MIRROR.

---

148 ELEPHANTS USE THEIR FEET TO HEAR LOW-FREQUENCY SOUNDS COMING THROUGH THE GROUND.

---

149 AN ELEPHANT'S TRUNK IS ACTUALLY A FUSION OF ITS NOSE AND ITS UPPER LIP.

---

150 ELEPHANTS HAVE THE LONGEST PREGNANCY OF ANY MAMMAL, LASTING NEARLY 22 MONTHS.

---

151 A SINGLE ELEPHANT TOOTH CAN WEIGH AS MUCH AS NINE POUNDS.

---

152 GIRAFFES HAVE BLACK TONGUES TO PREVENT THEM FROM GETTING SUNBURNED WHILE THEY EAT LEAVES.

153 A GROUP OF GIRAFFES IS CALLED A TOWER.

154 GIRAFFES ONLY NEED ABOUT 30 MINUTES OF SLEEP A DAY.

155 GIRAFFES HAVE THE SAME NUMBER OF NECK BONES AS HUMANS: SEVEN.

156 A GIRAFFE'S TONGUE CAN BE UP TO 20 INCHES LONG TO HELP IT STRIP LEAVES OFF TREES.

157 EACH ZEBRA'S STRIPE PATTERN IS UNIQUE, MUCH LIKE HUMAN FINGERPRINTS.

158 ZEBRA FOALS CAN WALK JUST 20 MINUTES AFTER THEY ARE BORN.

159 ZEBRAS ARE ACTUALLY BLACK WITH WHITE STRIPES, NOT WHITE WITH BLACK STRIPES.

160 A GROUP OF ZEBRAS IS CALLED A "DAZZLE".

161 ZEBRAS RUN IN A ZIGZAG PATTERN TO ESCAPE PREDATORS.

162 THE OKAPI LOOKS LIKE A ZEBRA, BUT IT IS ACTUALLY THE ONLY LIVING RELATIVE OF THE GIRAFFE.

163 HIPPOS HAVE SUCH THICK SKIN THAT THEY ARE VIRTUALLY BULLETPROOF.

164 HIPPOS CANNOT SWIM OR FLOAT; THEY TROT ALONG THE RIVER OR LAKE BED.

165 WHEN UNDERWATER, A HIPPO CAN HOLD ITS BREATH FOR UP TO FIVE MINUTES.

166 EVERY NIGHT, HIPPOS SPEND SIX HOURS EATING AN AVERAGE OF 88 POUNDS OF GRASS.

167 DESPITE THEIR SIZE, HIPPOS CAN RUN FASTER THAN HUMANS.

168 HIPPO SWEAT IS RED AND ACTS AS A NATURAL SUNSCREEN.

169 A GROUP OF HIPPOS IS CALLED A "BLOAT".

170 COWS PRODUCE MORE MILK WHEN THEY LISTEN TO SOOTHING MUSIC.

171 A SINGLE COW GIVES NEARLY 200,000 GLASSES OF MILK IN HER LIFETIME.

---

172 COWS HAVE ALMOST 360-DEGREE PANORAMIC VISION, ALLOWING THEM TO SEE PREDATORS COMING FROM ANY DIRECTION.

---

173 COWS CAN WALK UP STAIRS, BUT THEY CANNOT WALK DOWN THEM BECAUSE THEIR KNEES DON'T BEND THE RIGHT WAY.

---

174 COWS HAVE BEST FRIENDS AND GET STRESSED WHEN THEY ARE SEPARATED.

---

175 COWS HAVE NO UPPER FRONT TEETH; THEY USE A HARD DENTAL PAD TO HELP THEM CHEW GRASS.

---

176 A COW STANDS UP AND SITS DOWN ABOUT 14 TIMES A DAY.

---

177 PIGS DON'T SWEAT, WHICH IS WHY THEY ROLL IN MUD TO COOL THEMSELVES OFF.

---

178 PIGS ARE PHYSICALLY UNABLE TO LOOK UP INTO THE SKY.

---

179 PIGS ARE INTELLIGENT AND CAN PLAY VIDEO GAMES WITH JOYSTICKS.

180 PIGS ARE EXCELLENT SWIMMERS AND ENJOY COOLING OFF IN WATER.

181 MOST KANGAROOS ARE LEFT-HANDED.

182 THERE ARE MORE KANGAROOS THAN PEOPLE IN AUSTRALIA.

183 A KANGAROO USES ITS TAIL AS A THIRD LEG FOR BALANCE; IF YOU LIFT ITS TAIL, IT CANNOT HOP.

184 A BABY KANGAROO IS ABOUT THE SIZE OF A JELLYBEAN WHEN IT IS BORN.

185 A KANGAROO CAN JUMP 30 FEET IN A SINGLE BOUND.

186 KOALA FINGERPRINTS ARE ALMOST IDENTICAL TO HUMAN FINGERPRINTS.

187 KOALAS SLEEP FOR UP TO 22 HOURS A DAY.

188 KOALAS EAT ONLY EUCALYPTUS LEAVES, WHICH ARE POISONOUS TO ALMOST ALL OTHER ANIMALS.

189 KOALAS HAVE TWO THUMBS ON THEIR HANDS TO HELP THEM CLIMB.

---

190 A KOALA'S BRAIN IS COMPLETELY SMOOTH, UNLIKE A HUMAN BRAIN WHICH HAS FOLDS.

---

191 WOMBAT POOP IS SHAPED LIKE A CUBE TO STOP IT FROM ROLLING AWAY.

---

192 A WOMBAT'S POUCH FACES BACKWARD SO THEY DON'T SHOVEL DIRT INTO THEIR BABY'S FACE WHILE DIGGING.

---

193 WOMBATS USE THEIR TOUGHENED BACKSIDES TO BLOCK THEIR BURROWS AND CRUSH PREDATOR SKULLS AGAINST THE ROOF.

---

194 SLOTHS MOVE SO SLOWLY THAT ALGAE CAN GROW ON THEIR FUR, WHICH HELPS CAMOUFLAGE THEM IN THE TREES.

---

195 SLOTHS CAN HOLD THEIR BREATH LONGER THAN DOLPHINS CAN, UP TO 40 MINUTES UNDERWATER.

---

196 A SLOTH TAKES TWO WEEKS TO DIGEST A SINGLE MEAL.

---

197 SLOTHS CAN SWIM THREE TIMES FASTER THAN THEY CAN MOVE ON LAND.

198 SLOTHS ONLY POOP ONCE A WEEK AND LOSE UP TO ONE-THIRD OF THEIR BODY WEIGHT WHEN THEY DO.

199 PANDAS SPEND ABOUT 12 TO 14 HOURS EVERY DAY JUST EATING BAMBOO.

200 A GROUP OF PANDAS IS CALLED AN "EMBARRASSMENT".

201 GIANT PANDAS SOMETIMES FAKE BEING PREGNANT TO GET BETTER FOOD AND MORE ATTENTION FROM ZOOKEEPERS.

202 A RHINOCEROS HORN IS MADE OF COMPACTED HAIR, OR KERATIN, WHICH IS THE SAME MATERIAL AS YOUR FINGERNAILS.

203 A GROUP OF RHINOCEROS IS KNOWN AS A CRASH.

204 THE CAMEL'S LONG EYELASHES HELP KEEP DESERT SAND FROM BLOWING INTO ITS EYES.

205 CAMELS DO NOT STORE WATER IN THEIR HUMPS; THEY STORE FAT, WHICH THEY USE FOR ENERGY WHEN FOOD IS SCARCE.

206 CAMELS HAVE THREE EYELIDS TO PROTECT THEIR EYES FROM SAND.

207 A THIRSTY CAMEL CAN DRINK UP TO 40 GALLONS OF WATER IN JUST 10 MINUTES.

208 CAMELS CAN CLOSE THEIR NOSTRILS COMPLETELY TO KEEP SAND OUT DURING STORMS.

209 PLATYPUSES DO NOT HAVE STOMACHS.

210 MALE PLATYPUSES HAVE VENOMOUS SPURS ON THEIR FEET.

211 PLATYPUSES DO NOT HAVE NIPPLES; THEY SWEAT MILK OUT OF THEIR SKIN FOR THEIR BABIES TO LICK UP.

212 A GROUP OF PORCUPINES IS CALLED A PRICKLE.

213 PORCUPINES FLOAT IN WATER BECAUSE THEIR QUILLS ARE HOLLOW AND FILLED WITH AIR.

214 SOME CATS ARE ALLERGIC TO HUMANS.

215 CATS CAN SEE SIX TIMES BETTER AT NIGHT THAN HUMANS CAN.

216 CATS HAVE A THIRD EYELID.

217 CATS CAN MAKE OVER 100 DIFFERENT SOUNDS, WHILE DOGS CAN ONLY MAKE ABOUT 10.

218 CATS CANNOT TASTE SWEETNESS.

219 CATS SLEEP FOR 70% OF THEIR LIVES.

220 CATS HAVE 32 SEPARATE MUSCLES IN EACH OF THEIR EARS, ALLOWING THEM TO TURN THEIR EARS 180 DEGREES.

221 CATS USE THEIR WHISKERS TO MEASURE OPENINGS AND CHECK IF THEIR BODIES CAN FIT THROUGH THEM.

222 CATS CAN DRINK SEAWATER IF THEY HAVE TO BECAUSE THEIR KIDNEYS ARE EFFICIENT ENOUGH TO FILTER OUT THE SALT.

223 A CAT'S NOSE HAS A UNIQUE PATTERN OF RIDGES, JUST LIKE A HUMAN FINGERPRINT.

224 CATS HAVE A FREE-FLOATING COLLARBONE, WHICH ALLOWS THEM TO FIT THROUGH ANY SPACE THEIR HEAD CAN FIT THROUGH.

225 CATS HAVE FIVE TOES ON THEIR FRONT PAWS BUT ONLY FOUR ON THEIR BACK PAWS.

226 DOGS HAVE A SENSE OF TIME AND CAN TELL THE DIFFERENCE BETWEEN ONE HOUR AND FIVE HOURS.

227 THE NOSE PRINT OF A DOG IS UNIQUE, JUST LIKE A HUMAN FINGERPRINT.

228 A DOG'S SENSE OF SMELL IS ABOUT 40 TIMES BETTER THAN A HUMAN'S.

229 DALMATIANS ARE BORN COMPLETELY WHITE; THEIR SPOTS DEVELOP AS THEY GET OLDER.

230 BASENJI DOGS ARE THE ONLY BREED THAT CANNOT BARK; INSTEAD, THEY MAKE A YODEL SOUND.

231 DOGS SWEAT PRIMARILY THROUGH THEIR PAW PADS, NOT THEIR SKIN.

232 MALE PUPPIES WILL OFTEN LET FEMALE PUPPIES WIN WHEN THEY PLAY-FIGHT JUST TO BE POLITE.

233 ANCIENT HORSES WERE ABOUT THE SIZE OF DOGS.

234 HORSES CAN SLEEP STANDING UP BECAUSE THEIR LEGS CAN LOCK IN PLACE.

235 HORSES PHYSICALLY CANNOT VOMIT.

236 HORSES HAVE THE LARGEST EYES OF ANY LAND MAMMAL.

237 A HORSE'S TEETH TAKE UP MORE SPACE IN ITS HEAD THAN ITS BRAIN DOES.

238 HORSES CANNOT BREATHE THROUGH THEIR MOUTHS; THEY CAN ONLY BREATHE THROUGH THEIR NOSES.

239 IN SWITZERLAND, IT IS ILLEGAL TO OWN JUST ONE GUINEA PIG BECAUSE THEY GET LONELY.

240 GUINEA PIGS OFTEN SLEEP WITH THEIR EYES OPEN TO WATCH FOR PREDATORS.

241 RABBITS HAVE ALMOST TWICE AS MANY TASTE BUDS AS HUMANS HAVE.

242 A GROUP OF BUNNIES IS CALLED A "FLUFFLE".

243 RABBITS CAN SEE WHAT IS BEHIND THEM WITHOUT TURNING THEIR HEADS.

244 RABBITS CAN JUMP UP TO THREE FEET HIGH AND NINE FEET LONG IN A SINGLE LEAP.

245 HAMSTERS' TEETH NEVER STOP GROWING.

246 HAMSTERS CAN RUN UP TO EIGHT MILES ON THEIR WHEELS IN A SINGLE NIGHT.

247 SQUIRRELS PLANT THOUSANDS OF TREES EVERY YEAR JUST BY FORGETTING WHERE THEY HID THEIR NUTS.

248 SQUIRRELS FAKE BURYING NUTS TO TRICK THIEVES WHO MIGHT BE WATCHING THEM.

249 A FOX USES ITS TAIL TO COMMUNICATE WITH OTHER FOXES AND TO KEEP WARM IN WINTER.

250 FENNEC FOXES HAVE GIANT EARS THAT HELP RELEASE BODY HEAT SO THEY STAY COOL IN THE DESERT.

251 A BAT CAN EAT HUNDREDS OF MOSQUITOES IN ONE NIGHT.

252 BATS ARE THE ONLY MAMMALS THAT CAN FLY.

253 A CLOUD OF BATS IS CALLED A CAULDRON.

254 BAT LEG BONES ARE SO THIN AND LIGHT THAT NO BAT CAN WALK.

255 BATS ARE NOT BLIND; IN FACT, MANY BAT SPECIES CAN SEE BETTER THAN HUMANS.

256 ARMADILLO SHELLS ARE SO HARD THEY ARE EFFECTIVELY BULLETPROOF.

257 ARMADILLOS ALMOST ALWAYS GIVE BIRTH TO FOUR IDENTICAL BABIES.

258 THE EYES OF A REINDEER CHANGE COLOR FROM GOLD IN THE SUMMER TO BLUE IN THE WINTER.

259 REINDEER KNEES MAKE A CLICKING SOUND SO THE HERD CAN STAY TOGETHER DURING BLIZZARDS.

260 REINDEER ARE THE ONLY DEER SPECIES WHERE BOTH MALES AND FEMALES GROW ANTLERS.

261 A MOOSE'S ANTLERS CAN WEIGH AS MUCH AS A MICROWAVE.

262 A MOOSE CAN DIVE UNDERWATER DOWN TO 20 FEET TO EAT PLANTS AT THE BOTTOM OF A LAKE.

263 A GROUP OF MEERKATS IS CALLED A GANG OR MOB.

264 A GROUP OF LEMURS IS CALLED A "CONSPIRACY".

265 GIANT ANTEATERS HAVE NO TEETH.

266 CAPYBARAS ARE THE LARGEST RODENTS IN THE WORLD AND ARE EXCELLENT SWIMMERS.

267 SKUNKS CAN SPRAY THEIR SCENT UP TO 10 FEET AWAY.

268 SPOTTED SKUNKS DO A HANDSTAND BEFORE THEY SPRAY TO LOOK BIGGER AND SCARIER.

269 OPOSSUMS PLAY DEAD FOR HOURS WHEN THEY ARE SCARED, AND THEY EVEN EMIT A SMELL TO CONVINCE PREDATORS THEY ARE GONE.

270 HEDGEHOGS ARE IMMUNE TO SNAKE VENOM.

271 RATS MULTIPLY SO QUICKLY THAT IN 18 MONTHS, TWO RATS COULD THEORETICALLY HAVE OVER A MILLION DESCENDANTS.

272 RATS' TEETH NEVER STOP GROWING, SO THEY HAVE TO CHEW ON THINGS TO WEAR THEM DOWN.

273 NAKED MOLE RATS ARE IMMUNE TO CANCER AND CANNOT FEEL CERTAIN TYPES OF PAIN.

274 PANGOLINS ARE THE ONLY MAMMALS COVERED IN SCALES, WHICH ARE MADE OF KERATIN LIKE FINGERNAILS.

275 QUOKKAS ARE KNOWN AS THE "HAPPIEST ANIMAL ON EARTH" BECAUSE THEIR FACIAL STRUCTURE MAKES THEM LOOK LIKE THEY ARE SMILING.

276 THE TASMANIAN DEVIL IS NAMED AFTER THE FRIGHTENING SCREAM IT MAKES WHEN HUNTING AT NIGHT.

277 RED PANDAS STAND UP ON THEIR HIND LEGS TO LOOK BIGGER AND SCARIER WHEN THEY FEEL THREATENED.

278 THE NATIONAL ANIMAL OF AUSTRALIA IS THE RED KANGAROO.

279 SNOW LEOPARDS HAVE PAWS THAT ACT LIKE NATURAL SNOWSHOES TO KEEP THEM FROM SINKING INTO THE SNOW.

280 MOOSE ARE EXCELLENT SWIMMERS AND HAVE BEEN KNOWN TO SWIM UP TO TEN MILES WITHOUT STOPPING.

281 A GROUP OF PRAIRIE DOGS IS CALLED A TOWN.

282 A BABY ELEPHANT CAN DRINK UP TO THREE GALLONS OF MILK A DAY.

283 THE AFRICAN ELEPHANT HAS THE BEST SENSE OF SMELL IN THE ANIMAL KINGDOM.

284 REINDEER HAVE A SPECIAL LAYER OF TISSUE IN THEIR EYES THAT HELPS THEM SEE IN THE DARK ARCTIC WINTERS.

285 CHEETAHS CAN ACCELERATE FROM 0 TO 60 MILES PER HOUR IN JUST 3 SECONDS.

286 THE HONEY BADGER IS KNOWN AS THE WORLD'S MOST FEARLESS ANIMAL.

287 A WOMBAT'S TEETH NEVER STOP GROWING, SO THEY CHEW ON TOUGH GRASSES TO KEEP THEM FILED DOWN.

288 MOUNTAIN LIONS CAN JUMP 15 FEET HIGH INTO A TREE FROM A STANDSTILL.

289 THE MANED WOLF OF SOUTH AMERICA HAS A ROAR-BARK THAT SOUNDS LIKE A LARGE DOG COUGHING.

290 SLOTHS ARE SO SLOW THAT THEIR TOP SPEED ON THE GROUND IS JUST 10 FEET PER MINUTE.

291 AN ADULT MALE GORILLA CAN EAT UP TO 40 POUNDS OF VEGETATION IN A SINGLE DAY.

292 FOXES HAVE WHISKERS ON THEIR LEGS AS WELL AS THEIR FACES TO HELP THEM NAVIGATE IN TALL GRASS.

293 THE DEEPEST LIVING FISH EVER DISCOVERED WAS FOUND 27,000 FEET DOWN IN THE MARIANA TRENCH.

294 MORAY EELS HAVE A SECOND SET OF JAWS INSIDE THEIR THROAT THAT PULLS FOOD DOWN INTO THEIR STOMACH.

295 AN ADULT BLUE WHALE CAN EAT UP TO 40 MILLION KRILL IN A SINGLE DAY.

296 GIANT KELP CAN GROW UP TO TWO FEET A DAY UNDER THE RIGHT OCEAN CONDITIONS.

297 THE PORTUGUESE MAN O' WAR IS NOT A JELLYFISH, BUT A COLONY OF ORGANISMS WORKING TOGETHER.

---

298 MANTA RAYS ARE THE ONLY FISH KNOWN TO RECOGNIZE THEMSELVES IN A MIRROR.

---

299 THERE IS A SPECIES OF SNAIL THAT BUILDS A SHELL MADE OF IRON SULFIDE TO PROTECT ITSELF NEAR DEEP-SEA VENTS.

---

300 THE VAMPIRE SQUID DOES NOT SUCK BLOOD; IT EATS FLOATING OCEAN DEBRIS CALLED "MARINE SNOW".

---

301 DOLPHINS HAVE BEEN KNOWN TO USE SEA SPONGES AS TOOLS TO PROTECT THEIR SNOUTS WHILE FORAGING.

---

302 A SHARK'S SENSE OF SMELL IS SO POWERFUL IT CAN DETECT A SINGLE DROP OF BLOOD IN AN OLYMPIC-SIZED POOL.

---

303 AN ADULT WALRUS CAN WEIGH UP TO 3,000 POUNDS AND USES ITS TUSKS TO HAUL ITSELF ONTO ICE.

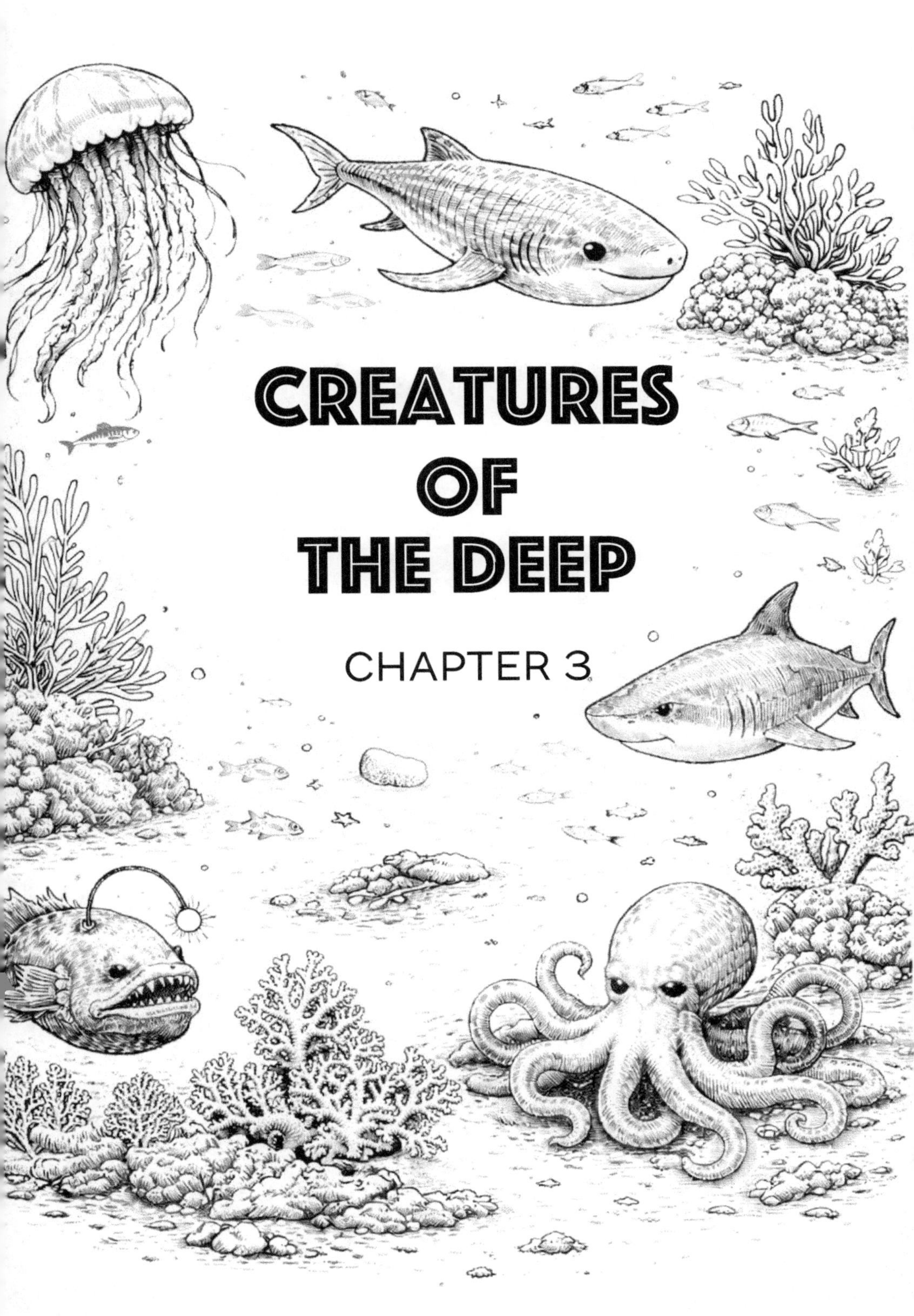

CREATURES OF THE DEEP

CHAPTER 3

304 A BLUE WHALE'S HEART IS THE SIZE OF A SMALL CAR.

---

305 THE BLUE WHALE IS BELIEVED TO BE THE LARGEST ANIMAL TO HAVE EVER LIVED ON THE PLANET.

---

306 YOU CAN HEAR A BLUE WHALE'S HEARTBEAT FROM TWO MILES AWAY.

---

307 BABY BLUE WHALES DRINK ABOUT 50 GALLONS OF MILK EVERY SINGLE DAY.

---

308 A BLUE WHALE'S TONGUE WEIGHS AS MUCH AS AN ENTIRE ADULT ELEPHANT.

---

309 THE CALL OF A BLUE WHALE IS LOUDER THAN A JET ENGINE AND CAN BE HEARD HUNDREDS OF MILES AWAY.

---

310 THE HEART OF A BLUE WHALE IS SO BIG THAT A HUMAN COULD SWIM THROUGH ITS ARTERIES.

---

311 A BLUE WHALE'S HEART ONLY BEATS ABOUT 8 TO 10 TIMES A MINUTE.

---

312 A BLUE WHALE'S SPRAY FROM ITS BLOWHOLE CAN SHOOT UP TO 30 FEET IN THE AIR.

313 SHARKS HAVE BEEN AROUND LONGER THAN TREES.

314 SHARKS DON'T HAVE BONES; THEIR SKELETONS ARE MADE ENTIRELY OF CARTILAGE.

315 MOST SHARKS WILL DROWN IF THEY STOP SWIMMING.

316 THERE ARE MORE THAN 500 SPECIES OF SHARK WORLDWIDE.

317 SHARKS LOSE TEETH THEIR ENTIRE LIVES AND CAN GROW UP TO 30,000 TEETH OVER A LIFETIME.

318 SHARKS ARE THE ONLY FISH THAT CAN BLINK WITH BOTH EYES.

319 SOME SHARKS GLOW IN THE DARK TO CAMOUFLAGE THEMSELVES FROM BELOW.

320 SHARKS HAVE SEVEN SENSES; THEY CAN DETECT ELECTRICITY IN THE WATER.

321 A GROUP OF SHARKS IS CALLED A "SHIVER".

322 SHARKS ARE IMMUNE TO ALMOST ALL KNOWN DISEASES.

323 SHARK SKIN FEELS LIKE SANDPAPER BECAUSE IT IS COVERED IN TINY TEETH-LIKE SCALES CALLED DERMAL DENTICLES.

324 GREENLAND SHARKS CAN LIVE TO BE OVER 400 YEARS OLD, MAKING THEM THE LONGEST-LIVING VERTEBRATES.

325 SHARKS HAVE BEEN KNOWN TO BITE UNDERWATER INTERNET CABLES BECAUSE THE ELECTRICITY THEY EMIT FEELS LIKE PREY.

326 WHEN A DOLPHIN SLEEPS, ONLY HALF OF ITS BRAIN GOES TO SLEEP, ALLOWING IT TO SURFACE FOR AIR.

327 DOLPHINS SHED THEIR SKIN ONCE EVERY TWO HOURS TO KEEP THEM SMOOTH AND SWIMMING EFFICIENTLY.

328 DOLPHINS THAT ARE CLOSELY BONDED MAY SWIM TOGETHER IN SYNCHRONY.

329 DOLPHINS SLEEP WITH ONE EYE OPEN.

330 DOLPHINS HAVE NAMES FOR EACH OTHER.

331 ORCAS, ALSO KNOWN AS KILLER WHALES, ARE ACTUALLY A TYPE OF DOLPHIN.

---

332 SPERM WHALES SLEEP VERTICALLY (STANDING UP) IN THE WATER, BOBBING LIKE GIANT LOGS.

---

333 SPERM WHALES CAN MAKE A SOUND SO LOUD IT COULD VIBRATE A HUMAN BODY TO DEATH.

---

334 BELUGA WHALES ARE KNOWN TO MIMIC HUMAN SPEECH.

---

335 NARWHALS CHANGE COLOR AS THEY GET OLDER; THEY START BLUE-GRAY AND END UP ALMOST COMPLETELY WHITE.

---

336 THE MALE NARWHAL'S LONG, SPIRAL TUSK IS ACTUALLY A TOOTH GROWING OUT OF ITS TOP LIP.

---

337 THE COLOSSAL SQUID, THE WORLD'S LARGEST INVERTEBRATE, HAS EYES THE SIZE OF BASKETBALLS.

---

338 THE GIANT SQUID HAS A DOUGHNUT-SHAPED BRAIN. EVERYTHING IT EATS PASSES THROUGH THE DOUGHNUT HOLE.

---

339 SQUIDS HAVE HARD BEAKS SIMILAR TO PARROTS.

340 AN OCTOPUS HAS THREE HEARTS. TWO PUMP BLOOD TO ITS GILLS, AND ONE PUMPS IT TO THE REST OF ITS BODY.

---

341 OCTOPUSES HAVE BLUE BLOOD BECAUSE THEY USE COPPER TO CARRY OXYGEN INSTEAD OF IRON.

---

342 A BABY OCTOPUS IS ABOUT THE SIZE OF A FLEA WHEN IT IS BORN.

---

343 AN OCTOPUS HAS NINE BRAINS: ONE CENTRAL BRAIN AND ONE IN EACH OF ITS EIGHT ARMS.

---

344 WHILE FLOATING ON THE OCEAN SURFACE, SEA OTTERS HOLD HANDS TO FORM LARGE COMMUNITIES CALLED RAFTS.

---

345 SEA OTTER POOP, CALLED SPRAINT, SMELLS LIKE HERBAL TEA.

---

346 SEA OTTERS HAVE A POCKET OF SKIN UNDER THEIR FOREARM WHERE THEY KEEP THEIR FAVORITE ROCK FOR CRACKING OPEN CLAMS.

---

347 SEA OTTERS WRAP THEMSELVES IN KELP SO THEY DON'T FLOAT AWAY WHILE THEY ARE SLEEPING.

---

348 SEA OTTERS HAVE THE DENSEST FUR OF ANY ANIMAL, WITH UP TO 1 MILLION HAIRS PER SQUARE INCH.

349 WALRUSES CAN SLEEP WHILE THEY ARE SWIMMING.

350 MANATEES CONTROL THEIR FLOATING BY STORING FARTS IN THEIR BODY.

351 STARFISH EAT BY TURNING THEIR STOMACHS INSIDE OUT AND WRAPPING THEM AROUND THEIR FOOD.

352 SEA STARS DON'T HAVE EYES; INSTEAD THEY HAVE AN EYE SPOT ON EACH ARM THAT SENSES LIGHT.

353 STARFISH DO NOT HAVE BLOOD; THEY PUMP SEAWATER THROUGH THEIR BODIES INSTEAD.

354 IF YOU CUT A STARFISH IN HALF, IT WON'T DIE; INSTEAD, IT MIGHT GROW INTO TWO NEW STARFISH.

355 THE IMMORTAL JELLYFISH CAN LIVE FOREVER, GROWING TO ADULTHOOD THEN REVERTING BACK TO ITS BABY STATE OVER AND OVER.

356 JELLYFISH HAVE NO HEART, BRAIN, BLOOD, OR SKELETON. THEY ARE ESSENTIALLY FLOATING STOMACHS.

357 SOME JELLYFISH CAN GLOW IN THE DARK, WHICH IS CALLED BIOLUMINESCENCE.

358 A GROUP OF JELLYFISH IS CALLED A "SMACK".

359 SEA SPONGES HAVE NO HEAD, MOUTH, EYES, FEELERS, BONES, HEART, LUNGS, OR BRAIN.

360 A SEA CUCUMBER EATS USING ITS FEET.

361 HORSESHOE CRAB BLOOD IS BRIGHT BLUE AND IS USED BY SCIENTISTS TO TEST FOR BACTERIA.

362 SEA HORSES ARE THE ONLY ANIMALS WHERE THE MALE GIVES BIRTH TO THE BABIES.

363 SEA HORSES MATE FOR LIFE AND HOLD TAILS WHEN THEY TRAVEL.

364 SEAHORSES ARE TERRIBLE SWIMMERS AND CAN DIE OF EXHAUSTION IN ROUGH WATER.

365 SEAHORSES HAVE NO STOMACHS, SO THEY HAVE TO EAT CONSTANTLY TO STAY ALIVE.

366 A SHRIMP'S HEART IS LOCATED IN ITS HEAD.

367 SHRIMP CAN SWIM BACKWARD.

368 THE PISTOL SHRIMP SNAPS ITS CLAW SO FAST IT CREATES A BUBBLE AS HOT AS THE SUN.

369 THE MANTIS SHRIMP CAN PUNCH WITH THE SPEED OF A .22 CALIBER BULLET, CREATING A SHOCKWAVE IN THE WATER.

370 LOBSTERS COMMUNICATE WITH EACH OTHER BY PEEING OUT OF THEIR FACES.

371 LOBSTERS TASTE FOOD WITH THEIR LEGS.

372 GIANT CLAMS ARE BIG ENOUGH FOR A HUMAN CHILD TO FIT INSIDE.

373 FISH CAN TASTE NOT ONLY IN THEIR MOUTHS, BUT ALSO ALL OVER THEIR BODIES.

374 CARNIVOROUS PIRANHAS WILL CLAMP DOWN ON GOATS THAT FALL INTO THE WATER.

375 AN OCEAN SUNFISH SOMETIMES FLOATS ON THE WATER'S SURFACE TO LET BIRDS PICK PARASITES OFF OF ITS BODY.

376 CLOWNFISH CAN CHANGE THEIR GENDER FROM MALE TO FEMALE.

377 CLOWNFISH ARE COATED IN A SPECIAL SLIME THAT MAKES THEM IMMUNE TO SEA ANEMONE STINGS.

378 A GROUP OF STINGRAYS IS CALLED A "FEVER".

379 IF YOU KEEP A GOLDFISH IN A DARK ROOM, IT WILL EVENTUALLY TURN PALE.

380 GOLDFISH ACTUALLY HAVE A MEMORY SPAN OF MONTHS, NOT JUST THREE SECONDS.

381 GOLDFISH DO NOT HAVE STOMACHS; THEY DIGEST FOOD IN THEIR INTESTINES AS THEY EAT.

382 THE WHALE SHARK IS THE LARGEST FISH IN THE OCEAN.

383 AN ELECTRIC EEL CAN GENERATE A SHOCK OF UP TO 600 VOLTS.

384 ELECTRIC EELS ARE NOT ACTUALLY EELS; THEY ARE A TYPE OF KNIFEFISH.

385 SOME FISH CAN COUGH TO CLEAR THEIR GILLS.

---

386 HAGFISH PRODUCE A SLIME THAT EXPANDS IN WATER TO CLOG THE GILLS OF PREDATORS.

---

387 PUFFERFISH CONTAIN A POISON THAT IS 1,200 TIMES DEADLIER THAN CYANIDE.

---

388 FLYING FISH CAN GLIDE OVER THE WATER FOR MORE THAN 600 FEET.

---

389 MUDSKIPPERS ARE FISH THAT CAN WALK ON LAND AND BREATHE AIR.

---

390 ARCHERFISH HUNT BY SHOOTING A STREAM OF WATER TO KNOCK BUGS OFF LEAVES.

---

391 STONEFISH ARE THE MOST VENOMOUS FISH IN THE WORLD.

---

392 PARROTFISH SLEEP INSIDE A BUBBLE OF MUCUS THEY MAKE THEMSELVES.

---

393 SWORDFISH HAVE A SPECIAL ORGAN THAT HEATS THEIR EYES SO THEY CAN SEE BETTER IN COLD WATER.

394 SALMON HAVE SUCH A GOOD SENSE OF SMELL THEY CAN FIND THEIR WAY BACK TO THE EXACT STREAM WHERE THEY WERE BORN.

---

395 A BABY FISH IS CALLED A "FRY".

---

396 THE BLOBFISH LOOKS NORMAL UNDERWATER; IT ONLY LOOKS DROOPY WHEN BROUGHT TO THE SURFACE BECAUSE OF THE PRESSURE CHANGE.

---

397 THERE IS A SPECIES OF SEA SLUG THAT CAN PHOTOSYNTHESIZE LIKE A PLANT.

---

398 OYSTERS CAN CHANGE THEIR GENDER BACK AND FORTH DEPENDING ON ENVIRONMENTAL CONDITIONS.

---

399 THE MIMIC OCTOPUS CAN SHAPE-SHIFT AND CHANGE COLORS TO LOOK LIKE DANGEROUS SEA CREATURES.

---

400 A BLUE WHALE'S BLOWHOLE IS LARGE ENOUGH FOR A TODDLER TO CRAWL INTO.

---

401 DEEP-SEA GIANT ISOPODS, WHICH LOOK LIKE MASSIVE PILL BUGS, CAN GO UP TO FIVE YEARS WITHOUT EATING A SINGLE MEAL.

---

402 A NAUTILUS CAN CONTROL HOW HIGH IT FLOATS IN THE WATER BY PUMPING GAS IN AND OUT OF THE EMPTY CHAMBERS IN ITS SHELL.

403 RIBBON WORMS CAN SHOOT A STICKY, WEB-LIKE TUBE OUT OF THEIR FACES TO TRAP THEIR FOOD.

404 A GROUP OF SEA TURTLES IS OFFICIALLY CALLED A "BALE".

405 FLOUNDER FISH ARE BORN WITH AN EYE ON EACH SIDE OF THEIR HEAD, BUT AS THEY GROW, ONE EYE MIGRATES SO BOTH ARE ON TOP.

406 THE FLAMBOYANT CUTTLEFISH IS THE ONLY CUTTLEFISH SPECIES THAT PREFERS TO WALK ALONG THE OCEAN FLOOR RATHER THAN SWIM.

407 MARINE IGUANAS ARE THE ONLY LIZARDS IN THE WORLD THAT DIVE INTO THE OCEAN TO FORAGE FOR FOOD.

408 THE OCEAN SUNFISH CAN LAY UP TO 300 MILLION EGGS AT A SINGLE TIME, MORE THAN ANY OTHER VERTEBRATE.

409 SEA SPONGES CAN COMPLETELY REBUILD THEIR BODIES EVEN IF THEY ARE SQUEEZED THROUGH A FINE MESH STRAINER.

410 SEA URCHINS USE THEIR FIVE SHARP TEETH TO CHEW THROUGH SOLID ROCK TO CREATE PERFECT HIDING SPOTS.

411 THE BARRELEYE FISH HAS A COMPLETELY TRANSPARENT, FLUID-FILLED HEAD THAT LETS IT LOOK STRAIGHT UP THROUGH ITS OWN FOREHEAD TO SPOT PREY.

BIRDS, BUGS & REPTILES

CHAPTER 4

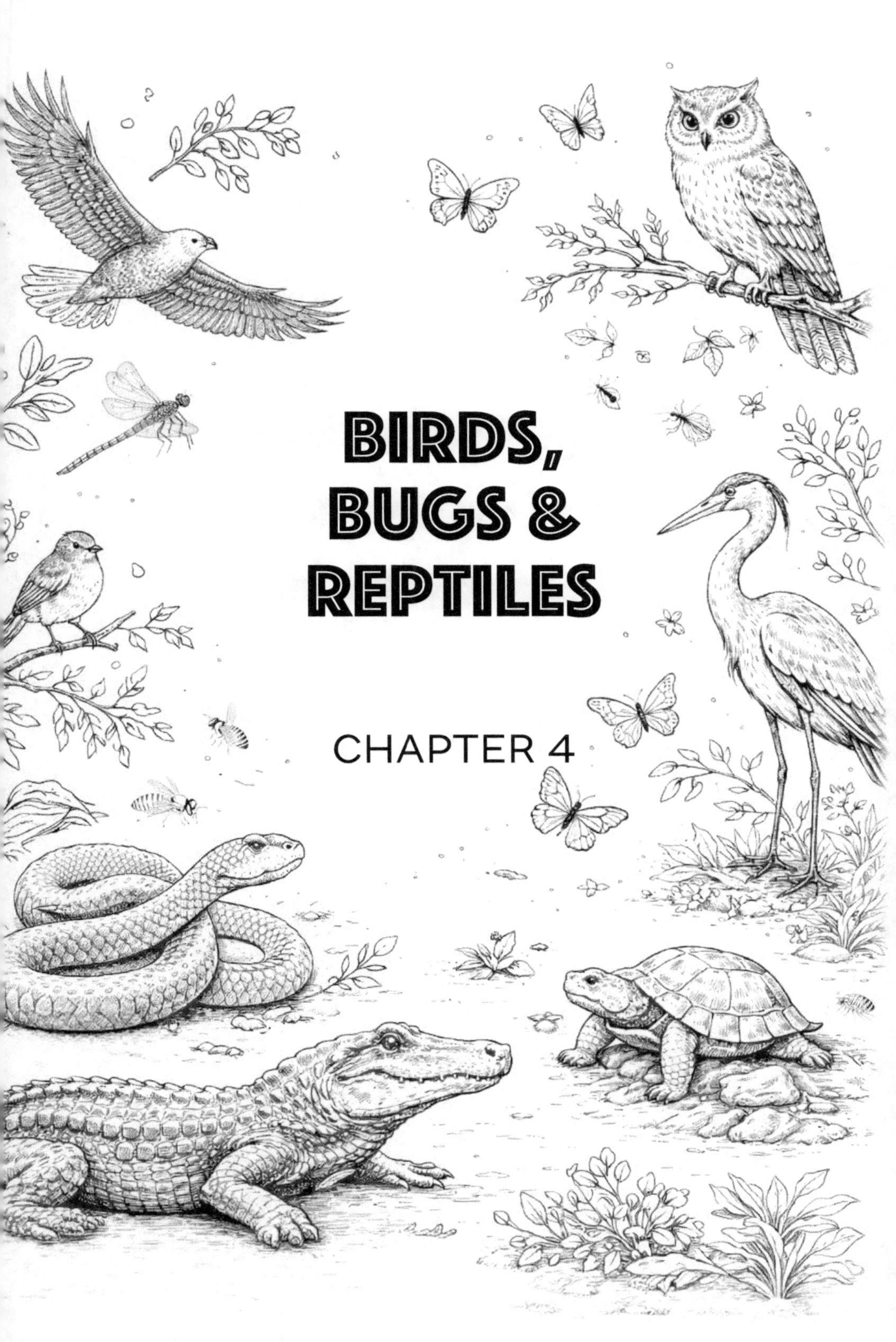

412 SPECIAL FEATHERS ON OWLS' WINGS MAKE THEIR FLIGHT NEARLY SILENT, SO THEY CAN SURPRISE PREY.

413 OWLS CAN TURN THEIR HEADS 270 DEGREES, WHICH IS ALMOST A FULL CIRCLE.

414 OWLS CANNOT MOVE THEIR EYES; THEY HAVE TO TURN THEIR HEADS.

415 A GROUP OF OWLS IS CALLED A "PARLIAMENT".

416 PENGUINS ARE THE ONLY BIRDS THAT CANNOT FOLD THEIR WINGS.

417 PENGUINS ARE DRAWN TO THE SCENT OF ROTTING EGGS.

418 GENTOO PENGUINS PROPOSE TO THEIR LIFE PARTNERS BY GIVING THEM A PEBBLE.

419 PENGUINS HAVE A SPECIAL GLAND ABOVE THEIR EYE THAT FILTERS SALT OUT OF THE OCEAN WATER THEY DRINK.

420 THE OSTRICH IS THE LARGEST BIRD IN THE WORLD. IT TYPICALLY STANDS AROUND SEVEN TO NINE FEET TALL.

421 OSTRICHES ARE THE ONLY TWO-TOED BIRDS.

---

422 AN OSTRICH'S KICK IS POWERFUL ENOUGH TO KILL A LION.

---

423 AN OSTRICH'S EYE IS BIGGER THAN ITS BRAIN.

---

424 OSTRICHES DO NOT BURY THEIR HEADS IN THE SAND; THEY LAY THEIR HEADS FLAT ON THE GROUND TO HIDE FROM PREDATORS.

---

425 FLAMINGOS ARE BORN WITH GRAY FEATHERS; THEY TURN PINK LATER BECAUSE OF THE SHRIMP THEY EAT.

---

426 A GROUP OF FLAMINGOS IS CALLED A "FLAMBOYANCE".

---

427 A FLAMINGO HAS TO EAT WITH ITS HEAD UPSIDE DOWN TO FILTER FOOD FROM THE WATER.

---

428 FLAMINGOS BEND THEIR LEGS AT THE ANKLE, NOT THE KNEE; THEIR ACTUAL KNEES ARE HIDDEN UP INSIDE THEIR FEATHERS.

---

429 A HUMMINGBIRD'S TONGUE IS SO LONG IT COILS INSIDE ITS HEAD.

430 THE BEE HUMMINGBIRD IS THE SMALLEST BIRD IN THE WORLD; IT IS SMALLER THAN A PENNY.

---

431 A HUMMINGBIRD'S HEART BEATS OVER 1,000 TIMES PER MINUTE.

---

432 A HUMMINGBIRD WILL STARVE TO DEATH IN ABOUT AN HOUR IF IT DOESN'T FIND FOOD BECAUSE ITS METABOLISM IS SO FAST.

---

433 HUMMINGBIRDS ARE THE ONLY BIRDS THAT CAN FLY BACKWARDS.

---

434 BIRD WINGS AND HUMAN ARMS HAVE THE SAME BONE STRUCTURE, BUT BIRDS CAN FLY AND HUMANS CAN'T.

---

435 A GROUP OF GEESE IS CALLED A GAGGLE WHEN THEY'RE ON THE GROUND, AND A SKEIN WHEN IN FLIGHT.

---

436 A GROUP OF CROWS IS CALLED A MURDER.

---

437 CROWS CAN HOLD GRUDGES AGAINST SPECIFIC PEOPLE WHO HAVE BEEN MEAN TO THEM.

---

438 CROWS OFTEN LEAVE GIFTS FOR PEOPLE WHO FEED THEM.

439 CROWS ARE SMART ENOUGH TO USE TOOLS, AND SOME EVEN DROP NUTS ON THE ROAD FOR CARS TO CRACK OPEN.

440 AN EAGLE CAN KILL A YOUNG DEER AND FLY AWAY WITH IT.

441 BALD EAGLES ARE NOT ACTUALLY BALD; THEIR NAME COMES FROM AN OLD ENGLISH WORD MEANING "WHITE-HEADED".

442 A FLOCK OF RAVENS IS CALLED AN "UNKINDNESS".

443 RAVENS CAN BE TAUGHT TO TALK AND CAN SOMETIMES MIMIC HUMAN SPEECH BETTER THAN PARROTS.

444 PUFFINS ARE OFTEN NICKNAMED THE "CLOWNS OF THE SEA".

445 A BABY PUFFIN IS CALLED A PUFFLING.

446 THE BEAK OF A PUFFIN GLOWS UNDER UV LIGHT.

447 THE PEREGRINE FALCON CAN DIVE AT SPEEDS OF OVER 200 MILES PER HOUR.

448 A WOODPECKER'S TONGUE WRAPS AROUND ITS BRAIN TO PROTECT IT FROM IMPACT WHILE PECKING.

449 WOODPECKERS HAVE SPECIAL SKULLS THAT ACT LIKE SHOCK ABSORBERS TO PROTECT THEIR BRAINS WHILE PECKING.

450 CHICKENS ARE THE CLOSEST LIVING RELATIVES TO THE T-REX.

451 THERE ARE MORE CHICKENS ON EARTH THAN PEOPLE.

452 TURKEYS CAN BLUSH; THE SKIN ON THEIR HEADS CHANGES COLOR WHEN THEY ARE EXCITED OR SICK.

453 PIGEONS CAN BE TRAINED TO DO SIMPLE MATH AND DISTINGUISH BETWEEN PAINTINGS BY DIFFERENT ARTISTS.

454 A BABY PIGEON IS CALLED A "SQUAB".

455 SWANS ARE ONE OF THE FEW BIRDS THAT MATE FOR LIFE.

456 A BABY SWAN IS CALLED A "CYGNET".

457 AN ALBATROSS CAN SLEEP WHILE IT IS FLYING.

458 ROBINS CAN EAT UP TO 14 FEET OF EARTHWORMS IN A SINGLE DAY.

459 THE COMMON SWIFT CAN STAY IN THE AIR FOR 10 MONTHS WITHOUT LANDING.

460 PEACOCKS ARE ACTUALLY JUST THE MALES; THE FEMALES ARE CALLED PEAHENS.

461 THE EXTINCT DODO BIRD WAS ACTUALLY A GIANT PIGEON.

462 THE DODO BIRD WENT EXTINCT LARGELY BECAUSE IT WAS NOT AFRAID OF HUMANS OR THE ANIMALS THEY BROUGHT WITH THEM.

463 THE SHOEBILL STORK CAN STAND PERFECTLY MOTIONLESS FOR HOURS WHILE HUNTING FISH.

464 THE KOOKABURRA BIRD IS FAMOUS BECAUSE ITS CALL SOUNDS EXACTLY LIKE A PERSON LAUGHING.

465 CASSOWARIES ARE CONSIDERED THE MOST DANGEROUS BIRDS IN THE WORLD BECAUSE OF THEIR DAGGER-LIKE CLAWS.

466 THE LYREBIRD CAN MIMIC ALMOST ANY SOUND, INCLUDING CHAINSAWS, CAMERA SHUTTERS, AND CAR ALARMS.

467 MAGPIES ARE THE ONLY NON-MAMMAL ANIMAL THAT CAN RECOGNIZE ITSELF IN A MIRROR.

468 ROOSTERS HAVE BUILT-IN "EARPLUGS" (FLAPS OF SKIN) THAT COVER THEIR EAR CANALS WHEN THEY CROW SO THEY DON'T DEAFEN THEMSELVES.

469 A MALE DUCK IS CALLED A "DRAKE".

470 EMUS AND KANGAROOS CANNOT WALK BACKWARD, WHICH IS WHY THEY APPEAR ON THE AUSTRALIAN COAT OF ARMS—TO SYMBOLIZE MOVING FORWARD.

471 ANTS NEVER SLEEP, AND THEY DO NOT HAVE LUNGS.

472 ANTS CAN CARRY OBJECTS THAT ARE 50 TIMES THEIR OWN BODY WEIGHT.

473 AN ANT'S SENSE OF SMELL IS STRONGER THAN A DOG'S.

474 THE TOTAL WEIGHT OF ALL THE ANTS ON EARTH IS ROUGHLY EQUAL TO THE WEIGHT OF ALL THE HUMANS.

475 THERE IS A SPECIES OF ANT CALLED THE "EXPLODING ANT" THAT EXPLODES TO PROTECT ITS COLONY.

476 A COCKROACH CAN LIVE FOR A WEEK WITHOUT ITS HEAD.

477 BEES CAN FLY HIGHER THAN MOUNT EVEREST.

478 HONEYBEES FLAP THEIR WINGS 200 TIMES EVERY SECOND.

479 HONEYBEES PERFORM A "WAGGLE DANCE" TO TELL OTHER BEES WHERE TO FIND FLOWERS.

480 BEES HAVE FIVE EYES: TWO LARGE ONES AND THREE SMALLER ONES ON TOP OF THEIR HEAD.

481 HONEYBEES CAN RECOGNIZE HUMAN FACES.

482 HONEYBEES HAVE HAIR ON THEIR EYES TO HELP THEM CATCH POLLEN.

483 HONEYBEES USUALLY DIE AFTER THEY STING A HUMAN BECAUSE THEIR STINGER GETS STUCK AND PULLS OUT THEIR ABDOMEN.

484 HONEYBEES CAN FLY AT SPEEDS OF UP TO 15 MILES PER HOUR.

485 A SINGLE HONEYBEE PRODUCES ONLY ABOUT 1/12TH OF A TEASPOON OF HONEY IN ITS ENTIRE LIFETIME.

486 TO MAKE JUST ONE POUND OF HONEY, A HIVE OF BEES MUST FLY A COMBINED DISTANCE OF 55,000 MILES.

487 SOME FLEAS CAN JUMP MORE THAN 150 TIMES THEIR HEIGHT.

488 PRAYING MANTIS FEMALES OFTEN EAT THEIR MATES, AND BABIES SOMETIMES EAT THEIR SIBLINGS.

489 FIREFLIES USE THEIR LIGHTS TO COMMUNICATE WITH EACH OTHER. DIFFERENT SPECIES HAVE DIFFERENT FLASHING PATTERNS.

490 MOSQUITOES USE INFRARED LIGHT TO FIND THE BEST AREAS ON AN ANIMAL'S BODY TO DRAW BLOOD.

491 MOSQUITOES ARE CONSIDERED THE DEADLIEST ANIMALS ON EARTH BECAUSE OF THE DISEASES THEY SPREAD.

492 ONLY FEMALE MOSQUITOES BITE; MALES JUST DRINK FLOWER NECTAR.

493 THE MONARCH BUTTERFLY WEIGHS LESS THAN A PAPERCLIP.

---

494 A BUTTERFLY'S EYE IS MADE OF THOUSANDS OF TINY LENSES.

---

495 BUTTERFLIES HAVE THEIR SKELETONS ON THE OUTSIDE OF THEIR BODIES (AN EXOSKELETON).

---

496 BUTTERFLIES TASTE WITH THEIR FEET.

---

497 A GROUP OF CATERPILLARS IS CALLED AN "ARMY".

---

498 A LADYBUG CAN EAT UP TO 5,000 OTHER BUGS IN ONE YEAR.

---

499 AROUND 2,000 SPECIES OF INSECTS ARE CONSIDERED EDIBLE FOR HUMANS.

---

500 CRICKETS AND GRASSHOPPERS CHIRP DIFFERENTLY DEPENDING ON THE TEMPERATURE.

---

501 ONLY MALE CRICKETS CHIRP.

502 CRICKETS HAVE WHITE BLOOD.

503 CRICKETS HAVE THEIR EARS LOCATED ON THEIR FRONT LEGS.

504 DRAGONFLIES HAVE SIX LEGS, BUT THEY CANNOT WALK.

505 DRAGONFLIES ARE THE MOST SUCCESSFUL HUNTERS IN NATURE, CATCHING 95% OF THE PREY THEY CHASE.

506 A HOUSEFLY HUMS IN THE MUSICAL KEY OF F.

507 A QUEEN TERMITE CAN LIVE TO BE 50 YEARS OLD.

508 TERMITES WILL EAT WOOD TWICE AS FAST IF THEY ARE LISTENING TO HEAVY METAL MUSIC.

509 DUNG BEETLES USE THE MILKY WAY GALAXY TO NAVIGATE AND ROLL THEIR DUNG BALLS IN A STRAIGHT LINE.

510 CICADAS ARE THE LOUDEST INSECTS IN THE WORLD; THEIR BUZZ CAN BE HEARD FROM A MILE AWAY.

511 INSECTS USE THEIR ANTENNAE TO SMELL AND TASTE THE WORLD AROUND THEM.

512 SCORPIONS GLOW UNDER BLACK LIGHT.

513 SCORPIONS CAN HOLD THEIR BREATH FOR UP TO SIX DAYS.

514 THE BLOOD OF SPIDERS IS CLEAR.

515 SPIDERS ARE ARACHNIDS, NOT INSECTS, BECAUSE THEY HAVE EIGHT LEGS AND TWO BODY PARTS.

516 THERE IS A SPECIES OF SPIDER THAT IS VEGETARIAN.

517 A SINGLE STRAND OF SPIDER SILK IS THINNER THAN A HUMAN HAIR BUT STRONGER THAN A PIECE OF STEEL OF THE SAME WIDTH.

518 SPIDER WEB SILK COMES OUT OF THE SPIDER AS A LIQUID AND HARDENS AS SOON AS IT TOUCHES THE AIR.

519 THERE IS A SPECIES OF SPIDER NAMED CALPONIA HARRISONFORDI AFTER ACTOR HARRISON FORD.

520 DADDY LONGLEGS ARE NOT TECHNICALLY SPIDERS; THEY ARE ARACHNIDS CALLED HARVESTMEN.

521 A TARANTULA CAN LIVE WITHOUT FOOD FOR MORE THAN TWO YEARS.

522 A SNAIL CAN SLEEP FOR UP TO THREE YEARS AT A TIME.

523 A SNAIL CAN GROW BACK A LOST EYE.

524 A GARDEN SNAIL CAN HAVE UP TO 14,000 TEETH.

525 A SNAIL BREATHES THROUGH A HOLE NEAR ITS HEAD CALLED A PNEUMOSTOME.

526 SLUGS ARE BOTH MALE AND FEMALE; THEY CAN FERTILIZE THEIR OWN EGGS.

527 SLUGS HAVE FOUR NOSES.

528 SOME WORMS CAN EAT THEMSELVES IF THEY CANNOT FIND FOOD.

529 WORMS CAN BREATHE THROUGH THEIR SKIN, BUT THEY MUST STAY MOIST TO DO IT.

---

530 AN EARTHWORM HAS FIVE HEARTS.

---

531 IF YOU CUT A PLANARIAN WORM IN HALF, IT WILL GROW TWO NEW HEADS, AND THE NEW HEAD WILL RETAIN THE MEMORIES OF THE ORIGINAL WORM.

---

532 EATING OR LICKING A POISON DART FROG CAN CAUSE ALMOST INSTANT DEATH.

---

533 POISON DART FROGS ARE NOT BORN POISONOUS; THEY GET THEIR TOXIN FROM THE BUGS THEY EAT IN THE RAINFOREST.

---

534 WHEN A NEWT LOSES OR DAMAGES A LEG, IT GROWS A NEW ONE.

---

535 WOOD FROGS FREEZE SOLID IN THE WINTER AND THAW OUT IN THE SPRING.

---

536 WOOD FROGS CAN HOLD THEIR PEE FOR UP TO EIGHT MONTHS.

---

537 FROGS CANNOT VOMIT; IF THEY NEED TO, THEY VOMIT THEIR ENTIRE STOMACH OUT OF THEIR MOUTH.

538 FROGS DRINK WATER THROUGH THEIR SKIN.

539 BULLFROGS DO NOT SLEEP.

540 FROGS USE THEIR EYEBALLS TO HELP THEM SWALLOW FOOD BY PUSHING THEM DOWN INTO THEIR THROAT.

541 GLASS FROGS HAVE TRANSPARENT SKIN ON THEIR BELLIES, SO YOU CAN SEE THEIR BEATING HEARTS.

542 A GROUP OF FROGS IS CALLED AN "ARMY".

543 THE "WOLVERINE FROG" BREAKS ITS OWN TOE BONES TO PUSH THEM THROUGH ITS SKIN AND USE THEM AS CLAWS.

544 AXOLOTLS CAN REGENERATE THEIR LIMBS, HEART, AND EVEN PARTS OF THEIR BRAIN.

545 A CHAMELEON'S TONGUE IS TWICE AS LONG AS ITS BODY.

546 THE WORLD'S SMALLEST REPTILE IS A CHAMELEON THAT FITS ON THE HEAD OF A MATCH.

547 SOME LIZARDS CAN DETACH THEIR TAILS TO ESCAPE PREDATORS, AND THEN GROW THEM BACK LATER.

---

548 LIZARDS CANNOT BREATHE AND RUN AT THE SAME TIME, SO THEY HAVE TO STOP TO CATCH THEIR BREATH.

---

549 THE THORNY DEVIL LIZARD DRINKS WATER BY STANDING IN PUDDLES AND LETTING THE WATER TRAVEL UP GROOVES IN ITS SKIN TO ITS MOUTH.

---

550 THERE IS A SPECIES OF LIZARD CALLED THE "HORNED LIZARD" THAT CAN SHOOT BLOOD FROM ITS EYES TO SCARE PREDATORS.

---

551 A CROCODILE CANNOT STICK ITS TONGUE OUT BECAUSE IT IS ATTACHED TO THE ROOF OF ITS MOUTH.

---

552 CROCODILES SWALLOW STONES TO INCREASE THEIR WEIGHT, WHICH HELPS THEM DIVE DEEPER.

---

553 ALLIGATORS CANNOT LIVE IN SALT WATER.

---

554 ALLIGATORS CAN SURVIVE IN FROZEN LAKES BY STICKING THEIR NOSES OUT OF THE ICE TO BREATHE WHILE THEIR BODIES HIBERNATE.

---

555 SEA TURTLES CRY TO REMOVE EXCESS SALT FROM THEIR BODIES.

556 SOME TURTLES CAN BREATHE THROUGH THEIR BUTTS.

557 TURTLES CAN FEEL IT WHEN YOU TOUCH THEIR SHELLS BECAUSE THEY HAVE NERVE ENDINGS IN THEM.

558 A TORTOISE NAMED JONATHAN IS THE OLDEST LIVING LAND ANIMAL; HE IS OVER 190 YEARS OLD.

559 A GROUP OF RATTLESNAKES IS CALLED A RHUMBA.

560 SNAKES CAN SENSE AN EARTHQUAKE COMING FROM 75 MILES AWAY, UP TO FIVE DAYS BEFORE IT HAPPENS.

561 A RATTLESNAKE'S RATTLE IS HOLLOW; THE SOUND COMES FROM THE SEGMENTS CLICKING TOGETHER, NOT THINGS SHAKING INSIDE.

562 SNAKES DO NOT HAVE EYELIDS, SO THEY CAN NEVER CLOSE THEIR EYES, EVEN WHEN THEY SLEEP.

563 FLYING SNAKES CAN GLIDE THROUGH THE AIR BY FLATTENING THEIR BODIES INTO A WING SHAPE.

564 THE TITANOBOA WAS A PREHISTORIC SNAKE THAT WAS AS LONG AS A SCHOOL BUS.

565 KOMODO DRAGONS HAVE VENOM GLANDS IN THEIR LOWER JAWS THAT HELP TAKE DOWN PREY.

566 GECKOS DO NOT HAVE EYELIDS; THEY LICK THEIR EYES TO KEEP THEM CLEAN.

567 PTERODACTYLS WERE NOT TECHNICALLY DINOSAURS; THEY WERE FLYING REPTILES.

568 A STEGOSAURUS HAD A BRAIN THE SIZE OF A WALNUT.

569 MANY DINOSAURS, INCLUDING THE T-REX, LIKELY HAD FEATHERS.

570 THE TYRANNOSAURUS REX LIVED CLOSER IN TIME TO HUMANS THAN IT DID TO THE STEGOSAURUS.

571 THE LONGEST RECORDED FLIGHT OF A CHICKEN IS 13 SECONDS.

572 A BABY SPIDER IS OFFICIALLY CALLED A "SPIDERLING".

573 THE FASTEST ANIMAL ON TWO LEGS IS THE OSTRICH, WHICH CAN SPRINT UP TO 45 MILES PER HOUR.

574 BUTTERFLIES CANNOT FLY IF THEIR BODY TEMPERATURE FALLS BELOW 86 DEGREES FAHRENHEIT.

575 A GROUP OF PARROTS IS CALLED A PANDEMONIUM.

576 THE HERCULES BEETLE CAN CARRY UP TO 850 TIMES ITS OWN BODY WEIGHT.

577 GECKOS USE MILLIONS OF TINY MICROSCOPIC HAIRS ON THEIR TOES TO CLIMB UP GLASS WALLS.

578 THE KING COBRA IS THE LONGEST VENOMOUS SNAKE IN THE WORLD, CAPABLE OF REACHING 18 FEET.

579 MOTHS DON'T HAVE NOSES; THEY USE THEIR FEATHERY ANTENNAE TO SMELL.

580 AN IGUANA CAN SURVIVE A FALL OF UP TO 40 FEET AND WALK AWAY UNHURT.

581 THE TONGUE OF A CHAMELEON IS SO FAST IT CAN SNATCH AN INSECT IN A FRACTION OF A SECOND.

582 A GROUP OF CROWS IS SO INTELLIGENT THEY CAN FIGURE OUT HOW TO DISPLACE WATER TO GET A FLOATING TREAT.

583 THE AMERICAN ALLIGATOR CAN GO THROUGH 3,000 TEETH IN ITS LIFETIME.

---

584 A DRAGONFLY CAN HOVER LIKE A HELICOPTER AND EVEN FLY BACKWARDS.

---

585 THE WANDERING ALBATROSS HAS THE LARGEST WINGSPAN OF ANY LIVING BIRD, STRETCHING OVER 11 FEET.

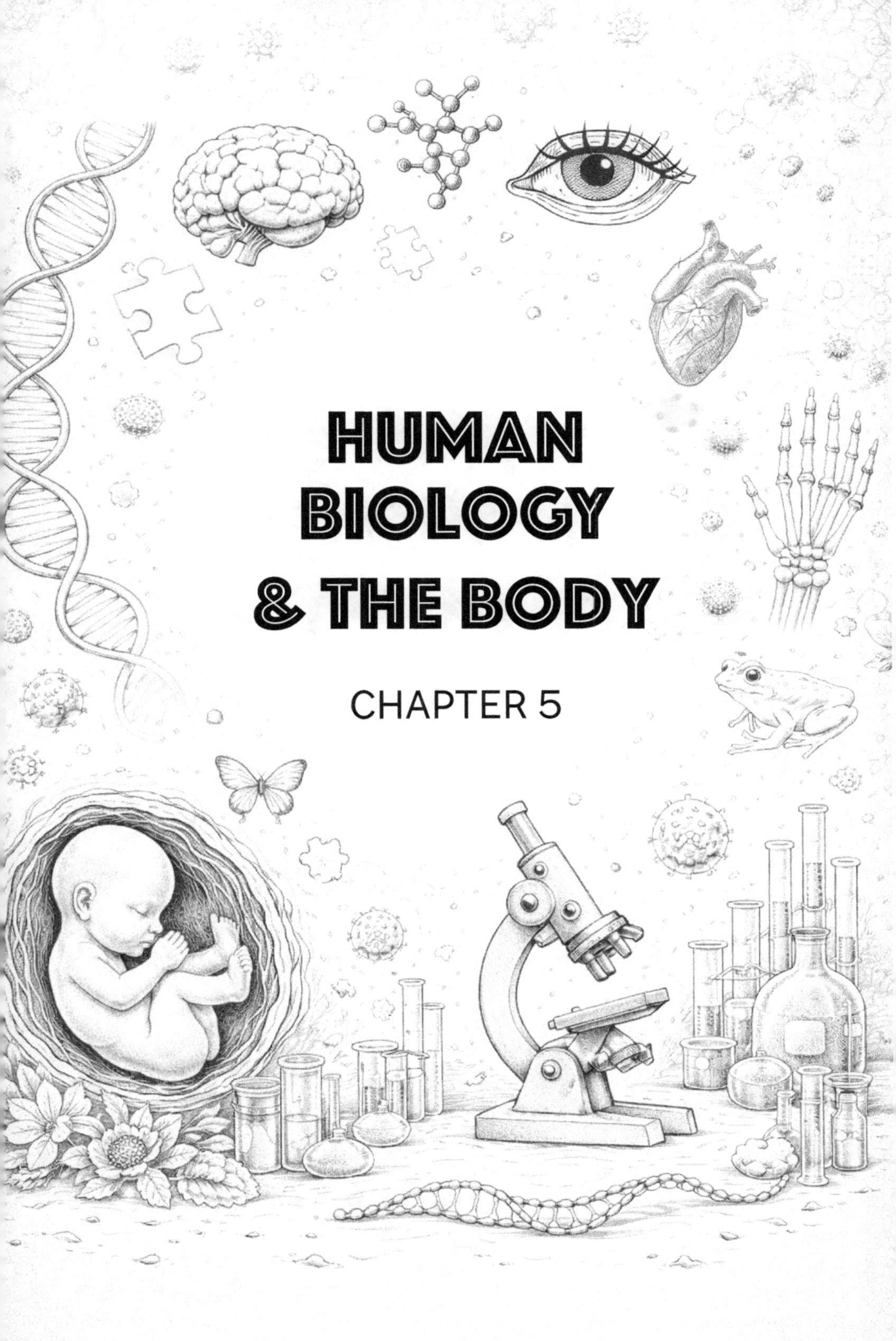
HUMAN
BIOLOGY
& THE BODY
CHAPTER 5

586 YOUR NOSE AND EARS NEVER STOP GROWING.

587 YOU CANNOT HUM WHILE HOLDING YOUR NOSE.

588 HUMANS SHARE 50% OF THEIR DNA WITH BANANAS.

589 YOU CAN DISTINGUISH A HOT WATER SPLASH FROM A COLD WATER SPLASH JUST BY THE SOUND.

590 HUMANS SNEEZE AT AROUND 100 MPH.

591 THE LONGEST BONE IN THE HUMAN BODY IS THE FEMUR (THIGHBONE).

592 BY AGE 60, THE AVERAGE PERSON HAS LOST HALF THE TASTE BUDS ON THEIR TONGUE.

593 A BABY'S EYES ARE ALMOST ADULT SIZE AT BIRTH, WHICH IS WHY THEY APPEAR LARGER THAN THE REST OF THEIR HEAD.

594 WHEN YOU BLUSH, THE LINING OF YOUR STOMACH DOES TOO.

595 THE AVERAGE PERSON PRODUCES ENOUGH SALIVA OVER THEIR LIFETIME TO FILL TWO SWIMMING POOLS.

596 IT'S NOT POSSIBLE TO TICKLE YOURSELF.

597 HUMANS CAN NAP WITH THEIR EYES OPEN.

598 THE HUMAN SKULL IS MADE UP OF 22 BONES.

599 BY THE AGE OF SIX, A HUMAN'S BRAIN IS ALREADY 90 PERCENT OF ITS ADULT SIZE.

600 SKIN IS THE BODY'S LARGEST ORGAN.

601 YOUR HEART BEATS 100,000 TIMES A DAY AND IS THE ONLY MUSCLE THAT NEVER RESTS.

602 ABOUT 60 PERCENT OF THE HUMAN BRAIN IS MADE OF FAT, MAKING IT THE FATTIEST ORGAN IN THE BODY.

603 ONE IN EVERY 2,000 BABIES IS BORN WITH A TOOTH ALREADY IN THEIR MOUTH.

604 HUMAN EYES BLINK AROUND 20 TIMES A MINUTE.

605 YOUR TONGUE HAS UNIQUE PATTERNS JUST LIKE YOUR FINGERPRINTS.

606 THERE IS NATURALLY A SMALL AMOUNT OF GOLD IN HUMAN BLOOD.

607 SNOT IS STICKY BECAUSE IT COLLECTS DEBRIS THAT GETS UP YOUR NOSE, TURNING INTO CRUMBLY BOOGERS.

608 DREAMS START WHEN WE ENTER REM (RAPID-EYE-MOVEMENT) SLEEP, ABOUT 90 MINUTES AFTER FALLING ASLEEP.

609 A HEALTHY PERSON CAN SURVIVE ONLY THREE DAYS WITHOUT WATER.

610 SUNLIGHT HELPS YOUR BODY PRODUCE VITAMIN D, WHICH CAN MAKE YOUR BONES AND MUSCLES STRONGER.

611 IT'S NOT POSSIBLE TO SNEEZE WITH YOUR EYES OPEN.

612 HANDWRITING IS GREAT EXERCISE FOR YOUR BRAIN. IT ENGAGES YOUR MEMORY, CREATIVITY, AND COGNITIVE FUNCTIONS.

613 IF YOU SNEEZE TOO HARD, YOU CAN ACTUALLY FRACTURE A RIB.

---

614 IF YOU LAID ALL THE BLOOD VESSELS IN A HUMAN CHILD END TO END, THEY WOULD CIRCLE THE EARTH TWICE.

---

615 THE AVERAGE PERSON WALKS THE EQUIVALENT OF FIVE TIMES AROUND THE WORLD IN THEIR LIFETIME.

---

616 THERE ARE MORE LIFEFORMS LIVING ON YOUR SKIN RIGHT NOW THAN THERE ARE PEOPLE ON THE PLANET.

---

617 HUMAN THIGH BONES ARE STRONGER THAN CONCRETE.

---

618 THE AVERAGE PERSON SPENDS ABOUT 25 YEARS OF THEIR LIFE SLEEPING.

---

619 YOUR FINGERNAILS GROW FOUR TIMES FASTER THAN YOUR TOENAILS.

---

620 WEARING HEADPHONES FOR JUST AN HOUR WILL INCREASE THE BACTERIA IN YOUR EAR BY 700 TIMES.

---

621 HUMAN TEETH ARE THE ONLY PART OF THE BODY THAT CANNOT HEAL THEMSELVES.

622 THE LONGEST TIME A PERSON HAS EVER HELD THEIR BREATH UNDERWATER IS OVER 24 MINUTES.

623 YOUR NOSE CAN REMEMBER 50,000 DIFFERENT SCENTS.

624 YOUR BRAIN GENERATES ENOUGH ELECTRICITY WHILE YOU ARE AWAKE TO POWER A SMALL LED LIGHTBULB.

625 THE ACID IN YOUR HUMAN STOMACH IS STRONG ENOUGH TO DISSOLVE METAL.

626 YOUR LEFT LUNG IS SLIGHTLY SMALLER THAN YOUR RIGHT LUNG TO MAKE ROOM FOR YOUR HEART.

627 HUMANS ACTUALLY GLOW WITH A FAINT LIGHT, BUT IT IS TOO WEAK FOR OUR EYES TO SEE.

628 THE SMALLEST BONE IN THE HUMAN BODY IS INSIDE YOUR EAR AND IS THE SIZE OF A GRAIN OF RICE.

629 BABIES ARE BORN WITH ABOUT 300 BONES, BUT ADULTS ONLY HAVE 206 BECAUSE SOME FUSE TOGETHER.

630 YOUR FEET CONTAIN ABOUT 250,000 SWEAT GLANDS.

631 RED IS THE RAREST NATURAL HAIR COLOR IN THE WORLD.

632 MOST OF THE DUST IN YOUR HOUSE IS ACTUALLY MADE OF DEAD SKIN CELLS.

633 "BRAIN FREEZE" IS A WARNING SIGNAL FROM YOUR BODY TO STOP EATING COLD FOOD SO YOUR BRAIN DOESN'T GET TOO COLD.

634 THE HUMAN BRAIN IS COMPOSED OF ABOUT 75% WATER.

635 THE FASTEST MUSCLE IN YOUR BODY IS THE ONE THAT MAKES YOU BLINK.

636 HUMANS SHED ABOUT 40 POUNDS OF SKIN IN THEIR LIFETIME.

637 EARWAX IS ACTUALLY A TYPE OF SWEAT.

638 FINGERNAILS GROW FASTER ON YOUR DOMINANT HAND.

639 HUMANS ARE THE ONLY ANIMALS THAT HAVE CHINS.

640 THE "BLOOD" IN YOUR VEINS IS NEVER BLUE; IT IS ALWAYS RED, BUT IT LOOKS BLUE THROUGH YOUR SKIN BECAUSE OF HOW LIGHT TRAVELS.

---

641 YOUR SKELETON COMPLETELY RENEWS ITSELF EVERY 10 YEARS.

---

642 YOUR BRAIN USES ABOUT 20% OF ALL THE OXYGEN AND BLOOD IN YOUR BODY.

---

643 HUMANS ARE THE ONLY ANIMALS THAT BLUSH.

---

644 THE TONGUE IS THE ONLY MUSCLE IN THE HUMAN BODY THAT IS ATTACHED AT ONLY ONE END.

---

645 THE TALLEST MAN IN RECORDED HISTORY, ROBERT WADLOW, WAS 8 FEET 11 INCHES TALL.

---

646 THE LONGEST MUSCLE IN THE HUMAN BODY IS THE SARTORIUS, WHICH RUNS FROM YOUR HIP TO YOUR KNEE.

---

647 TOOTH ENAMEL IS THE HARDEST SUBSTANCE IN THE HUMAN BODY, EVEN HARDER THAN BONE.

---

648 HUMAN HAIR GROWS FASTER IN THE SUMMER THAN IT DOES IN THE WINTER.

649 BEARDS GROW FASTER THAN ANY OTHER HAIR ON THE HUMAN BODY.

650 THE LENGTH OF YOUR THUMB IS GENERALLY THE SAME AS THE LENGTH OF YOUR NOSE.

651 THE CORNEA (THE CLEAR FRONT PART OF YOUR EYE) IS THE ONLY PART OF THE BODY THAT HAS NO BLOOD VESSELS; IT GETS OXYGEN DIRECTLY FROM THE AIR.

652 HUMAN BABIES BLINK ONLY ONCE OR TWICE A MINUTE, WHILE ADULTS BLINK MUCH MORE OFTEN.

653 YOU USE ABOUT 200 DIFFERENT MUSCLES JUST TO TAKE A SINGLE STEP.

654 YAWNING HELPS COOL DOWN YOUR BRAIN.

655 ONLY ABOUT 10% OF THE WORLD'S POPULATION IS LEFT-HANDED.

656 MOST PEOPLE BREATHE THROUGH ONE NOSTRIL AT A TIME, SWITCHING SIDES EVERY FEW HOURS.

657 THE SOUND OF CRACKING YOUR KNUCKLES IS ACTUALLY GAS BUBBLES BURSTING IN YOUR JOINTS.

658 GOOSEBUMPS ARE A LEFTOVER TRAIT FROM WHEN OUR ANCESTORS HAD MORE HAIR; PUFFING UP THE HAIR HELPED KEEP THEM WARM OR LOOK BIGGER TO ENEMIES.

---

659 NERVE IMPULSES TRAVEL TO AND FROM THE BRAIN AT SPEEDS OF UP TO 170 MILES PER HOUR.

---

660 THE HUMAN BRAIN ITSELF CANNOT FEEL PAIN BECAUSE IT HAS NO PAIN RECEPTORS.

---

661 YOUR HEART IS ABOUT THE SAME SIZE AS YOUR FIST.

---

662 YOUR LIVER IS THE ONLY INTERNAL ORGAN THAT CAN COMPLETELY REGENERATE ITSELF.

---

663 WATCHING HORROR MOVIES CAN BURN CALORIES BECAUSE YOUR HEART RATE INCREASES SIGNIFICANTLY.

---

664 YOUR NOSE IS ALWAYS VISIBLE TO YOUR EYES, BUT YOUR BRAIN IGNORES IT SO IT DOESN'T DISTRACT YOU.

---

665 YOUR EARS POP IN AIRPLANES BECAUSE THE AIR PRESSURE OUTSIDE CHANGES FASTER THAN THE AIR INSIDE YOUR EARS CAN ADJUST.

---

666 HICCUPS ARE CAUSED BY A SUDDEN SPASM IN YOUR DIAPHRAGM MUSCLE.

667 IF YOU SMOOTHED OUT ALL THE WRINKLES IN YOUR BRAIN, IT WOULD BE ABOUT THE SIZE OF A PILLOWCASE.

---

668 HUMAN TEETH ARE JUST AS STRONG AS SHARK TEETH.

---

669 HUMANS ARE THE ONLY SPECIES ON EARTH THAT CRY EMOTIONAL TEARS.

---

670 BLUE EYES ARE ACTUALLY A GENETIC MUTATION; ORIGINALLY, ALL HUMANS HAD BROWN EYES.

---

671 NEWBORN BABIES DON'T SHED TEARS WHEN THEY CRY UNTIL THEY ARE AT LEAST ONE MONTH OLD.

---

672 HAIR AND NAILS DO NOT KEEP GROWING AFTER DEATH; THE SKIN AROUND THEM JUST SHRINKS, MAKING THEM LOOK LONGER.

---

673 YOUR LITTLE FINGER CONTRIBUTES ABOUT 50% OF YOUR HAND'S OVERALL STRENGTH.

---

674 YOUR BRAIN IS MORE ACTIVE WHEN YOU ARE SLEEPING THAN WHEN YOU ARE WATCHING TV.

---

675 ONE-QUARTER OF ALL THE BONES IN YOUR BODY ARE LOCATED IN YOUR FEET.

676 YOUR BLOOD IS ROUGHLY AS SALTY AS THE OCEAN.

677 YOUR SMALL INTESTINE IS ABOUT 22 FEET LONG—IF YOU STRETCHED IT OUT, IT WOULD BE LONGER THAN A CAR.

678 HUMANS BLINK MORE FREQUENTLY WHEN THEY ARE TALKING.

679 YOUR NOSE ACTS AS A HEATER TO WARM UP COLD AIR BEFORE IT REACHES YOUR SENSITIVE LUNGS.

680 THE SPACE BETWEEN YOUR EYEBROWS IS CALLED THE GLABELLA.

681 THE GROOVE BETWEEN YOUR NOSE AND UPPER LIP IS CALLED THE PHILTRUM.

682 THE WHITE CRESCENT SHAPE AT THE BASE OF YOUR FINGERNAIL IS CALLED THE LUNULE.

683 YOUR TASTE BUDS ARE REPLACED EVERY 10 TO 14 DAYS.

684 YOU ARE TEMPORARILY PARALYZED DURING DEEP SLEEP SO YOU DON'T ACT OUT YOUR DREAMS.

685 INFORMATION TRAVELS THROUGH YOUR NERVES AT ABOUT 250 MILES PER HOUR.

---

686 A COUGH CAN TRAVEL OUT OF YOUR MOUTH AT 50 MILES PER HOUR.

---

687 YOUR HEART HAS ITS OWN ELECTRICAL IMPULSE AND CAN CONTINUE TO BEAT EVEN IF SEPARATED FROM THE BODY.

---

688 THE SMALL INTESTINE IS NAMED "SMALL" BECAUSE IT IS NARROW, NOT BECAUSE IT IS SHORT.

---

689 YOUR JAW MUSCLES CAN BITE DOWN WITH 200 POUNDS OF FORCE.

---

690 THE HYOID BONE IN YOUR THROAT IS THE ONLY BONE IN THE BODY NOT CONNECTED TO ANOTHER BONE.

---

691 THE GLUTEUS MAXIMUS IS THE LARGEST MUSCLE IN THE HUMAN BODY.

---

692 IT TAKES FEWER MUSCLES TO SMILE THAN IT DOES TO FROWN.

---

693 IDENTICAL TWINS HAVE DIFFERENT FINGERPRINTS.

694 BLONDES NATURALLY HAVE MORE HAIR STRANDS THAN BRUNETTES.

---

695 REDHEADS OFTEN REQUIRE MORE ANESTHESIA DURING SURGERY THAN PEOPLE WITH OTHER HAIR COLORS.

---

696 BROWN EYES ARE ACTUALLY BLUE EYES COVERED IN A LAYER OF BROWN PIGMENT.

---

697 YOU PRODUCE ABOUT A LITER OF MUCUS EVERY SINGLE DAY.

---

698 YOUR EYES HAVE A RESOLUTION OF APPROXIMATELY 576 MEGAPIXELS.

---

699 IF YOU UNRAVELED ALL THE DNA IN YOUR BODY, IT WOULD STRETCH FROM PLUTO TO THE SUN AND BACK.

---

700 THE "FUNNY BONE" IS NOT A BONE AT ALL; IT IS THE ULNAR NERVE BUMPING AGAINST YOUR HUMERUS BONE.

---

701 MOST PEOPLE CANNOT LICK THEIR OWN ELBOWS.

---

702 YOUR HEART PUMPS ABOUT 2,000 GALLONS OF BLOOD EVERY SINGLE DAY.

703 HUMANS HAVE A TAILBONE (THE COCCYX), WHICH IS A LEFTOVER FROM WHEN OUR ANCESTORS HAD TAILS.

704 ONLY ABOUT 10-20% OF PEOPLE CAN WIGGLE THEIR EARS.

705 HETEROCHROMIA IS A CONDITION WHERE A PERSON HAS TWO DIFFERENT COLORED EYES.

706 "SPHENOPALATINE GANGLIONEURALGIA" IS THE SCIENTIFIC MEDICAL TERM FOR "BRAIN FREEZE".

707 "BORBORYGMUS" IS THE MEDICAL TERM FOR THE RUMBLING SOUND YOUR STOMACH MAKES.

708 "HORRIPILATION" IS THE TECHNICAL WORD FOR GETTING GOOSEBUMPS.

709 THE "TRAGUS" IS THE NAME OF THE LITTLE BUMP OF CARTILAGE ON THE INSIDE OF YOUR EAR.

710 THE "PURLICUE" IS THE SPACE BETWEEN YOUR THUMB AND YOUR FOREFINGER.

711 THE LINES ON THE INSIDE OF YOUR WRIST ARE CALLED "RASCETA".

712 THE FLESHY PART OF THE NOSE BETWEEN YOUR NOSTRILS IS CALLED THE "COLUMELLA NASI".

713 THE "SMELL OF OLD PEOPLE" IS A DISTINCT SCENT CAUSED BY A CHEMICAL COMPOUND CALLED 2-NONENAL.

714 YOUR STOMACH LINING REPLACES ITSELF EVERY 3 TO 4 DAYS TO PREVENT THE ACID FROM DIGESTING YOUR STOMACH.

715 YOU ARE TALLER IN THE MORNING THAN IN THE EVENING BECAUSE GRAVITY COMPRESSES YOUR SPINE DURING THE DAY.

716 THE STRONGEST MUSCLE IN THE HUMAN BODY (BY WEIGHT) IS THE MASSETER (JAW MUSCLE).

717 BABIES ARE BORN WITHOUT KNEECAPS; THEY HAVE CARTILAGE THAT TURNS INTO BONE LATER.

718 YOU LOSE UP TO 30% OF YOUR TASTE BUDS DURING AN AIRPLANE FLIGHT BECAUSE OF THE HIGH ALTITUDE AND DRY AIR.

719 IT IS PHYSICALLY IMPOSSIBLE TO BREATHE AND SWALLOW AT THE EXACT SAME TIME.

720 HUMAN BONES ARE ABOUT FIVE TIMES STRONGER THAN STEEL OF THE EXACT SAME DENSITY.

721 YOUR BLOOD MAKES UP ABOUT 8% OF YOUR TOTAL BODY WEIGHT.

---

722 AN ADULT HUMAN BODY CONTAINS AROUND 100,000 MILES OF BLOOD VESSELS.

---

723 HUMANS SHARE ABOUT 1% TO 2% OF THEIR DNA WITH NEANDERTHALS.

---

724 THE HUMAN EYE CAN BLINK IN JUST A TENTH OF A SECOND.

---

725 YOUR BODY CONTAINS ENOUGH IRON TO MAKE A 3-INCH NAIL.

---

726 BABIES ARE BORN WITH ABOUT 10,000 TASTE BUDS, WHILE ADULTS HAVE CLOSER TO 5,000.

---

727 HUMANS ARE THE ONLY ANIMALS CAPABLE OF DRAWING A PERFECTLY STRAIGHT LINE.

---

728 THE HUMAN EYE CAN DISTINGUISH BETWEEN ROUGHLY 10 MILLION DIFFERENT COLORS.

---

729 YOU PRODUCE ENOUGH HEAT IN 30 MINUTES TO BOIL A HALF-GALLON OF WATER.

730 YOUR THUMB HAS ITS OWN PULSE.

---

731 YOUR BODY PRODUCES A NEW TOP LAYER OF SKIN EVERY 30 DAYS.

EARTH SCIENCE & NATURE

CHAPTER 6

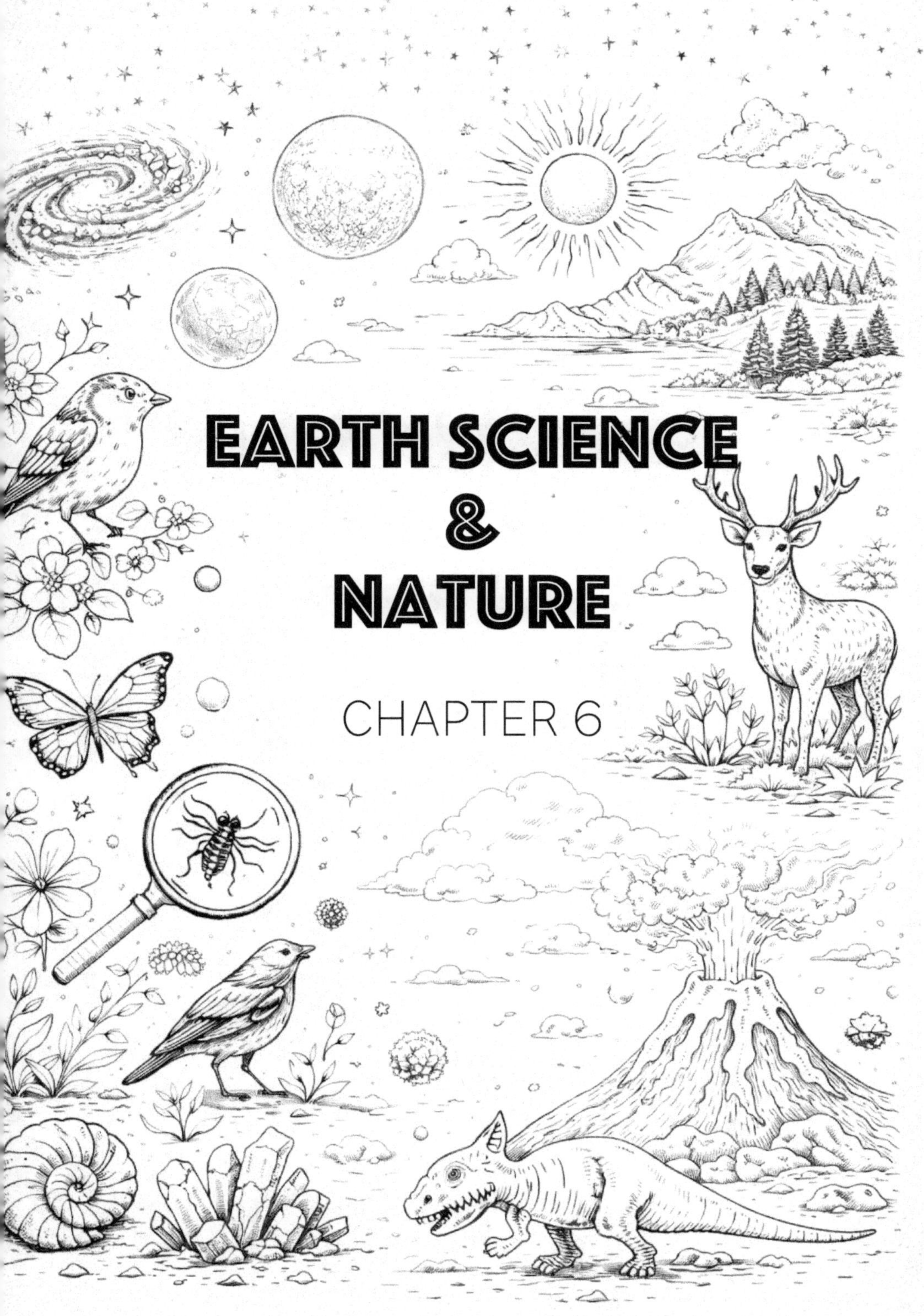

732 ONLY 5% OF THE OCEAN HAS BEEN EXPLORED.

---

733 THE WORLD'S TALLEST VOLCANO, MAUNA LOA IN HAWAII, STANDS AT 13,677 FEET.

---

734 OAK TREES ARE STRUCK BY LIGHTNING MORE OFTEN THAN ANY OTHER TREE SPECIES.

---

735 LIGHTNING CAN JUMP FROM AN OBJECT TO A PERSON.

---

736 FOREST FIRES MOVE MORE QUICKLY UPHILL THAN DOWNHILL.

---

737 ANTARCTICA WAS COMPLETELY ICE-FREE UNTIL ABOUT 34 MILLION YEARS AGO.

---

738 ANIMALS CAN OFTEN SENSE NATURAL DISASTERS BEFORE HUMANS DO.

---

739 THE ONLY CONTINENT WITH NO ACTIVE VOLCANOES IS AUSTRALIA.

---

740 RAINDROPS ARE SHAPED MORE LIKE HAMBURGER BUNS THAN TEARDROPS.

741 THE HIMALAYAS GROW ABOUT 0.4 INCHES (1 CM) TALLER EVERY YEAR.

---

742 AROUND THE WORLD, LIGHTNING STRIKES 50 TO 100 TIMES EVERY SECOND.

---

743 LIMESTONE IS MADE OF SEASHELLS AND CAN BE FOUND IN PLACES THAT WERE ONCE COVERED BY OCEANS.

---

744 VENUS FLYTRAPS EAT BUGS TO OBTAIN NUTRIENTS THAT ARE NOT AVAILABLE IN WETLAND SOIL.

---

745 THE OCEAN FLOOR IS NOT FLAT; IT HAS HILLS, MOUNTAINS, PLAINS, AND THE WORLD'S DEEPEST VALLEYS.

---

746 WHEN IRON IS STRUCK BY LIGHTNING, IT CAN BECOME A LODESTONE—THE ONLY NATURALLY OCCURRING MAGNET.

---

747 THIRTY PERCENT OF THE EARTH IS COVERED IN FORESTS.

---

748 THE WORD "SAHARA" MEANS DESERT IN ARABIC, SO THE SAHARA DESERT IS LITERALLY THE DESERT DESERT.

---

749 EIGHTY PERCENT OF THE WORLD'S PLANTS AND ANIMALS ARE FOUND IN FORESTS.

750 THE WORLD'S OLDEST ISLAND IS MADAGASCAR.

751 THE HOTTEST TEMPERATURE EVER RECORDED WAS 134°F IN DEATH VALLEY, CALIFORNIA.

752 WINDS INSIDE A TORNADO CAN REACH SPEEDS OF MORE THAN 300 MPH.

753 MORE THAN 18.5 PERCENT OF THE WORLD'S MOST POWERFUL EARTHQUAKES TAKE PLACE IN JAPAN.

754 THE PACIFIC OCEAN COVERS 60 MILLION SQUARE MILES, MAKING IT THE WORLD'S LARGEST OCEAN.

755 ICE IS LIGHTER THAN WATER, WHICH IS WHY IT FLOATS.

756 EVERY SNOWFLAKE IS UNIQUE.

757 MORE THAN HALF OF THE OXYGEN WE BREATHE COMES FROM SEAWEED AND PLANT PLANKTON IN THE OCEAN.

758 SOME ISLANDS ARE HUMAN-MADE.

759 THE GREAT BARRIER REEF IS THE LARGEST LIVING STRUCTURE ON EARTH AND IS VISIBLE FROM SPACE.

760 A CLOUD CAN ZIP ACROSS THE SKY AT 100 MILES PER HOUR.

761 A CUBIC MILE OF FOG CONTAINS LESS THAN A GALLON OF WATER.

762 YOU CAN FLOAT EASILY IN THE DEAD SEA BECAUSE THE WATER IS INCREDIBLY SALTY.

763 IF MEASURED FROM ITS UNDERWATER BASE, MAUNA KEA IN HAWAII IS TALLER THAN MOUNT EVEREST.

764 IN 1811, AN EARTHQUAKE WAS SO POWERFUL IT CAUSED THE MISSISSIPPI RIVER TO FLOW BACKWARD.

765 ANTARCTICA IS TECHNICALLY THE LARGEST DESERT IN THE WORLD BECAUSE IT GETS SO LITTLE PRECIPITATION.

766 ONLY 3% OF THE WATER ON EARTH IS FRESH WATER; THE REST IS SALTWATER.

767 TREES CAN COMMUNICATE WITH EACH OTHER USING A NETWORK OF UNDERGROUND FUNGI.

768 THE CONTINENTS MOVE AT ABOUT THE SAME SPEED THAT YOUR FINGERNAILS GROW.

---

769 THE DEAD SEA IS SINKING ABOUT ONE METER EVERY YEAR.

---

770 THE AMAZON RAINFOREST PRODUCES ABOUT 20% OF THE WORLD'S OXYGEN.

---

771 THERE IS A WATERFALL IN ANTARCTICA CALLED "BLOOD FALLS" THAT OOZES RED WATER BECAUSE IT IS RICH IN IRON.

---

772 SOUND TRAVELS ABOUT FOUR TIMES FASTER IN WATER THAN IT DOES IN THE AIR.

---

773 THE MARIANA TRENCH IN THE PACIFIC OCEAN IS SO DEEP THAT MOUNT EVEREST COULD FIT INSIDE IT WITH MILES TO SPARE.

---

774 CLOUDS LOOK WHITE BECAUSE THEY REFLECT SUNLIGHT; RAIN CLOUDS LOOK DARK BECAUSE THEY ARE SO THICK SUNLIGHT CAN'T PASS THROUGH.

---

775 A LIGHTNING BOLT IS ABOUT 54,000 DEGREES FAHRENHEIT, WHICH IS FIVE TIMES HOTTER THAN THE SURFACE OF THE SUN.

---

776 A BOLT OF LIGHTNING CONTAINS ENOUGH ENERGY TO TOAST 100,000 SLICES OF BREAD.

777 THE WATER IN THE ATLANTIC OCEAN IS SALTIER THAN THE WATER IN THE PACIFIC OCEAN.

---

778 THE LOCH NESS IN SCOTLAND HOLDS MORE FRESH WATER THAN ALL THE LAKES IN ENGLAND AND WALES COMBINED.

---

779 MOUNT EVEREST IS TECHNICALLY STILL GROWING ABOUT 4 MILLIMETERS EVERY YEAR DUE TO TECTONIC PLATES SHIFTING.

---

780 A SINGLE BOLT OF LIGHTNING IS ABOUT AN INCH WIDE.

---

781 THE NORTHERN LIGHTS ARE CAUSED BY SOLAR WIND HITTING EARTH'S ATMOSPHERE.

---

782 THUNDER IS THE SOUND OF AIR EXPANDING RAPIDLY BECAUSE OF THE HEAT FROM LIGHTNING.

---

783 HURRICANES SPIN COUNTER-CLOCKWISE IN THE NORTHERN HEMISPHERE AND CLOCKWISE IN THE SOUTHERN HEMISPHERE.

---

784 THE "EYE" OF A HURRICANE IS ACTUALLY THE CALMEST PART OF THE STORM.

---

785 SNOW IS NOT ACTUALLY WHITE; IT IS TRANSLUCENT, BUT IT LOOKS WHITE BECAUSE OF HOW LIGHT REFLECTS OFF IT.

786 HAILSTONES CAN SOMETIMES GROW TO BE THE SIZE OF GRAPEFRUITS.

787 WILDFIRES CAN GET SO BIG THAT THEY CREATE THEIR OWN WEATHER SYSTEMS.

788 THE PACIFIC OCEAN IS SLOWLY SHRINKING, WHILE THE ATLANTIC OCEAN IS GROWING.

789 THERE IS ENOUGH GOLD SUSPENDED IN THE OCEAN'S WATER TO GIVE EVERY PERSON ON EARTH 9 POUNDS OF IT.

790 CORAL REEFS ARE ACTUALLY MADE OF ANIMALS, NOT PLANTS.

791 SUNLIGHT CAN PENETRATE THE OCEAN TO A DEPTH OF ABOUT 3,300 FEET; BELOW THAT, IT IS TOTAL DARKNESS.

792 THERE ARE NO RIVERS IN SAUDI ARABIA.

793 THE DRIEST PLACE ON EARTH IS THE ATACAMA DESERT IN CHILE.

794 SOUND TRAVELS 15 TIMES FASTER THROUGH STEEL THAN IT DOES THROUGH THE AIR.

795 CHALK IS ACTUALLY MADE FROM BILLIONS OF TINY FOSSILIZED PLANKTON.

796 OBSIDIAN IS A NATURAL GLASS FORMED BY VOLCANOES.

797 DIAMONDS ARE THE HARDEST NATURAL SUBSTANCE ON EARTH.

798 THE SARGASSO SEA IS THE ONLY SEA IN THE WORLD THAT HAS NO COASTLINE; IT IS BOUNDED ENTIRELY BY OCEAN CURRENTS.

799 ANTARCTICA HOLDS ABOUT 70% OF THE WORLD'S FRESH WATER.

800 THE SMELL OF RAIN HITTING DRY GROUND IS CALLED PETRICHOR.

801 CHIMBORAZO IN ECUADOR IS THE CLOSEST POINT ON EARTH TO OUTER SPACE, NOT MOUNT EVEREST.

802 MAWSYNRAM, INDIA, IS THE WETTEST PLACE ON EARTH.

803 THE OLDEST LIVING TREE IS OVER 4,800 YEARS OLD.

804 THE TALLEST TREE IN THE WORLD IS A REDWOOD NAMED HYPERION, STANDING 380 FEET TALL.

805 A VENUS FLYTRAP CAN "COUNT" TO ENSURE AN INSECT IS INSIDE BEFORE SNAPPING SHUT.

806 THE "CORPSE FLOWER" BLOOMS VERY RARELY AND SMELLS LIKE ROTTING MEAT.

807 GIANT AMAZON WATER LILIES ARE STRONG ENOUGH TO SUPPORT THE WEIGHT OF A SMALL CHILD.

808 MOUNT THOR IN CANADA HAS THE WORLD'S GREATEST VERTICAL DROP.

809 THE SMELL OF FRESHLY CUT GRASS IS ACTUALLY A DISTRESS SIGNAL FROM THE PLANTS.

810 THE EARTH IS NOT A PERFECT SPHERE; IT BULGES SLIGHTLY AT THE EQUATOR BECAUSE OF HOW FAST IT SPINS.

811 THE NILE RIVER FLOWS NORTH, UNLIKE MOST OTHER MAJOR RIVERS THAT FLOW SOUTH.

812 NIAGARA FALLS ACTUALLY STOPPED FLOWING ONCE IN 1848 DUE TO A MASSIVE ICE BLOCKAGE.

813 FULGURITES ARE "FOSSILIZED LIGHTNING" FORMED WHEN LIGHTNING STRIKES SAND AND MELTS IT INTO GLASS.

---

814 THE WORLD'S LARGEST RECORDED SNOWFLAKE WAS 15 INCHES WIDE.

---

815 THERE ARE SAILING STONES IN DEATH VALLEY, CALIFORNIA, THAT MOVE ACROSS THE GROUND ON THEIR OWN.

---

816 THE SAHARA DESERT WAS ONCE A LUSH, GREEN RAINFOREST THOUSANDS OF YEARS AGO.

---

817 A "SUN DOG" IS A WEATHER PHENOMENON THAT MAKES IT LOOK LIKE THERE ARE THREE SUNS IN THE SKY.

---

818 LAKE MARACAIBO IN VENEZUELA HAS THE MOST LIGHTNING IN THE WORLD, WITH STORMS 300 NIGHTS A YEAR.

---

819 A "FIRE RAINBOW" IS A RARE CLOUD PHENOMENON THAT LOOKS LIKE A RAINBOW MADE OF FLAMES.

---

820 THERE ARE UNDERWATER RIVERS IN THE OCEAN THAT HAVE THEIR OWN TREES AND LEAVES.

---

821 THE GROUND IN THE ATACAMA DESERT IS SO SIMILAR TO MARS THAT NASA TESTS ITS ROVERS THERE.

822 THERE IS A CAVE IN MEXICO FILLED WITH CRYSTALS THE SIZE OF TELEPHONE POLES.

823 THE DEEPEST PART OF THE OCEAN IS CALLED THE CHALLENGER DEEP.

824 THE GREAT BLUE HOLE IS A GIANT UNDERWATER SINKHOLE OFF THE COAST OF BELIZE.

825 A CLOUD CAN WEIGH MORE THAN A MILLION POUNDS.

826 THE SAHARA DESERT ACTUALLY SNOWS ABOUT ONCE EVERY 30 YEARS.

827 MOUNT EVEREST CONTAINS MARINE FOSSILS (LIKE SEASHELLS) AT ITS PEAK BECAUSE IT USED TO BE AT THE BOTTOM OF THE OCEAN.

828 THE GRAND CANYON IS BIG ENOUGH TO HOLD THE ENTIRE WORLD'S POPULATION.

829 THE DEEPEST LAKE IN THE WORLD, LAKE BAIKAL IN RUSSIA, HOLDS 20% OF THE WORLD'S UNFROZEN FRESH WATER.

830 LAKE HILLIER IN AUSTRALIA IS NATURALLY BRIGHT PINK, LOOKING LIKE STRAWBERRY MILK.

831 THERE IS A "DOOR TO HELL" IN TURKMENISTAN, A CRATER THAT HAS BEEN BURNING WITH NATURAL GAS FOR OVER 50 YEARS.

---

832 POINT NEMO IS THE SPOT IN THE OCEAN FARTHEST FROM ANY LAND. THE CLOSEST HUMANS ARE OFTEN THE ASTRONAUTS ON THE SPACE STATION.

---

833 THE ATLANTIC OCEAN IS GETTING WIDER BY ABOUT ONE INCH EVERY YEAR.

---

834 A SUNFLOWER IS NOT JUST ONE FLOWER; THE CENTER IS MADE OF HUNDREDS OF TINY FLOWERS.

---

835 BAMBOO IS THE FASTEST-GROWING PLANT IN THE WORLD AND CAN GROW UP TO 35 INCHES IN A SINGLE DAY.

---

836 THE AMAZON RAINFOREST IS SO LARGE THAT IT CREATES ITS OWN WEATHER SYSTEM AND RAIN.

---

837 A "KING TIDE" IS AN EXCEPTIONALLY HIGH TIDE THAT HAPPENS WHEN THE SUN AND MOON ALIGN PERFECTLY.

---

838 THERE IS A SPECIES OF PALM TREE THAT CAN "WALK" BY GROWING NEW ROOTS AND LETTING OLD ONES DIE.

---

839 A "MOONBOW" IS A RAINBOW PRODUCED BY MOONLIGHT INSTEAD OF SUNLIGHT.

840 THE FASTEST GUST OF WIND EVER RECORDED ON THE SURFACE OF THE EARTH WAS 253 MILES PER HOUR.

---

841 MOST OF THE EARTH'S OXYGEN ISN'T PRODUCED BY TREES, BUT BY MICROSCOPIC OCEAN PLANTS CALLED PHYTOPLANKTON.

---

842 A TYPICAL HURRICANE PRODUCES THE ENERGY EQUIVALENT OF 10,000 NUCLEAR BOMBS.

---

843 HAWAII IS THE ONLY U.S. STATE THAT IS GEOGRAPHICALLY LOCATED IN OCEANIA, NOT NORTH AMERICA.

---

844 THERE IS AN UNDERGROUND RIVER BENEATH THE AMAZON RIVER CALLED THE HAMZA RIVER.

---

845 THE EARTH'S MAGNETIC FIELD ACTS AS A GIANT SHIELD, PROTECTING THE PLANET FROM HARMFUL SOLAR RADIATION.

---

846 A TSUNAMI CAN TRAVEL ACROSS THE OCEAN AT SPEEDS OF UP TO 500 MILES PER HOUR, AS FAST AS A JET PLANE.

---

847 THE LONGEST MOUNTAIN RANGE ON EARTH IS ACTUALLY ENTIRELY UNDERWATER, CALLED THE MID-OCEAN RIDGE.

---

848 THE GRAND PRISMATIC SPRING IN YELLOWSTONE GETS ITS BRILLIANT RAINBOW COLORS FROM HEAT-LOVING BACTERIA.

849 THERE IS ENOUGH WATER IN LAKE SUPERIOR TO COVER ALL OF NORTH AND SOUTH AMERICA IN A FOOT OF WATER.

---

850 A SINGLE MATURE OAK TREE CAN DROP UP TO 10,000 ACORNS IN A SINGLE YEAR.

---

851 PEAT BOGS STORE MORE CARBON THAN ALL THE WORLD'S FORESTS COMBINED.

---

852 DUST FROM THE SAHARA DESERT IS BLOWN ACROSS THE ATLANTIC OCEAN AND ACTUALLY FERTILIZES THE AMAZON RAINFOREST.

---

853 ABOUT 90% OF THE WORLD'S FRESHWATER IS LOCKED UP IN THE ICE SHEETS OF ANTARCTICA AND GREENLAND.

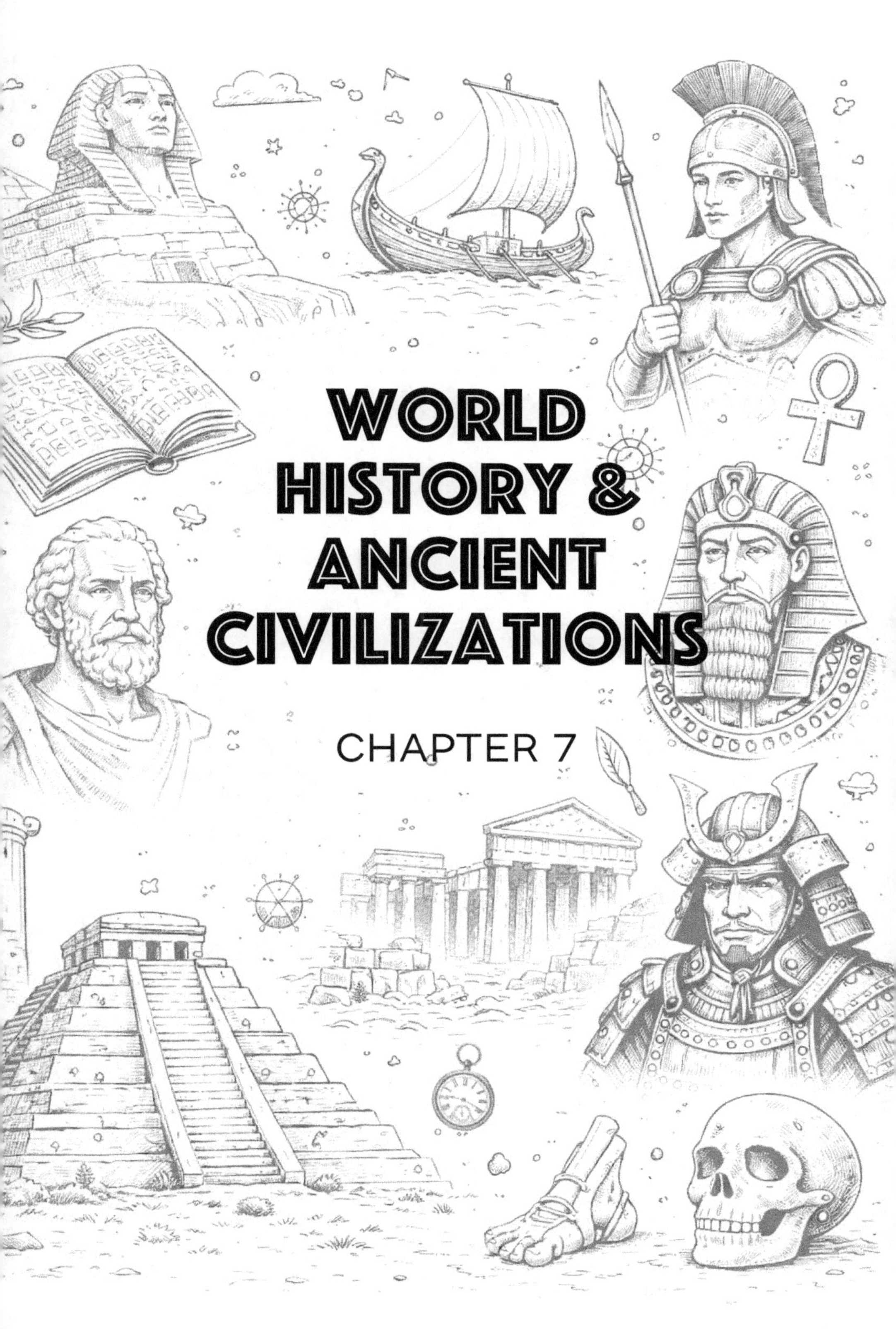

WORLD HISTORY & ANCIENT CIVILIZATIONS

CHAPTER 7

854 OXFORD UNIVERSITY IS OLDER THAN THE AZTEC EMPIRE.

---

855 CLEOPATRA LIVED CLOSER IN TIME TO THE INVENTION OF THE IPHONE THAN TO THE BUILDING OF THE GREAT PYRAMIDS.

---

856 MAMMOTHS WERE STILL ALIVE WHEN THE GREAT PYRAMIDS WERE BEING BUILT.

---

857 THE ANCIENT ROMANS USED THEIR PEE AS MOUTHWASH.

---

858 ANCIENT ROMANS USED CRUSHED OYSTER SHELLS AND BONES AS TOOTHPASTE.

---

859 THE FIRST MARSHMALLOWS WERE MADE BY THE ANCIENT EGYPTIANS.

---

860 MUMMIES HAVE BEEN FOUND ON EVERY CONTINENT.

---

861 KING TUTANKHAMUN HAD A DAGGER MADE FROM A METEORITE.

---

862 THE WORD "GYMNASIUM" COMES FROM THE GREEK WORD "GYMNOS," WHICH MEANS NAKED, BECAUSE ANCIENT GREEKS EXERCISED NAKED.

863 THE COLOSSEUM IN ROME USED TO BE FLOODED WITH WATER SO THEY COULD STAGE NAVAL SEA BATTLES.

864 THE SHORTEST WAR IN HISTORY WAS BETWEEN BRITAIN AND ZANZIBAR IN 1896; ZANZIBAR SURRENDERED AFTER 38 MINUTES.

865 THE SHORTEST REIGNING MONARCH IN HISTORY WAS KING LOUIS XIX OF FRANCE, WHO WAS KING FOR ONLY 20 MINUTES.

866 KNIGHTS USUALLY BEGAN THEIR TRAINING BY THE TIME THEY WERE SEVEN YEARS OLD.

867 CASTLE FLOORS WERE RARELY SWEPT; MESSES WERE OFTEN COVERED WITH STRAW AND FLOWERS.

868 IN CASTLES, HAY WAS USED AS TOILET PAPER.

869 DEFENDERS OF CASTLES DUMPED BOILING WATER AND HOT SAND ON ATTACKERS FROM ABOVE.

870 MOATS WERE OFTEN USED AS CASTLE GARBAGE DUMPS AND A PLACE FOR EMPTYING TOILETS.

871 HENRY III, THE MEDIEVAL KING OF ENGLAND, ONCE KEPT A POLAR BEAR AS A PET AT THE TOWER OF LONDON.

872 VIKINGS DID NOT WEAR HORNED HELMETS; THAT WAS AN IDEA ADDED BY COSTUME DESIGNERS IN OPERA.

873 LEONARDO DA VINCI COULD WRITE WITH ONE HAND WHILE DRAWING WITH THE OTHER.

874 EARLY CANNONS COULD ONLY BE FIRED TEN TIMES AN HOUR AS THEIR BARRELS HAD TO COOL DOWN BETWEEN SHOTS.

875 THE GREAT WALL OF CHINA IS NOT ACTUALLY VISIBLE FROM SPACE WITH THE NAKED EYE.

876 STICKY RICE WAS USED AS A SUPER-STRONG MORTAR TO BUILD PARTS OF THE GREAT WALL OF CHINA.

877 THE BRITISH MONARCH LEGALLY OWNS ONE-SIXTH OF THE EARTH'S LAND SURFACE.

878 GEORGE WASHINGTON, THE FIRST UNITED STATES PRESIDENT, NEVER LIVED AT THE WHITE HOUSE.

879 GEORGE WASHINGTON DIED BEFORE THE FIRST DINOSAUR FOSSIL WAS SCIENTIFICALLY IDENTIFIED.

880 JAMES A. GARFIELD WAS THE FIRST LEFT-HANDED US PRESIDENT.

881 TWO PEANUT FARMERS HAVE BEEN ELECTED PRESIDENT IN THE UNITED STATES: THOMAS JEFFERSON AND JIMMY CARTER.

---

882 ANDREW JACKSON'S PET PARROT HAD TO BE REMOVED FROM JACKSON'S FUNERAL BECAUSE IT WOULDN'T STOP SCREAMING SWEAR WORDS.

---

883 PRESIDENT JOHN QUINCY ADAMS HAD A PET ALLIGATOR THAT HE KEPT IN A BATHTUB AT THE WHITE HOUSE.

---

884 ABRAHAM LINCOLN GREW HIS FAMOUS BEARD BECAUSE AN 11-YEAR-OLD GIRL WROTE HIM A LETTER SAYING HIS FACE WAS TOO THIN.

---

885 ABRAHAM LINCOLN IS IN THE WRESTLING HALL OF FAME; HE ONLY LOST ONE MATCH OUT OF APPROXIMATELY 300.

---

886 ABRAHAM LINCOLN USED TO KEEP IMPORTANT DOCUMENTS AND MAIL INSIDE HIS TALL HAT.

---

887 PRESIDENT ULYSSES S. GRANT WAS ONCE ARRESTED FOR SPEEDING ON HIS HORSE.

---

888 THE WHITE HOUSE HAS A PRIVATE BOWLING ALLEY, A MOVIE THEATER, AND A CHOCOLATE SHOP.

---

889 THE LIBERTY BELL HAS A TYPO ON IT; THE WORD "PENNSYLVANIA" IS SPELLED "PENSYLVANIA".

890 BENJAMIN FRANKLIN WANTED THE NATIONAL BIRD OF THE UNITED STATES TO BE A TURKEY, NOT A BALD EAGLE.

891 THE TORCH OF THE STATUE OF LIBERTY HAS BEEN CLOSED TO VISITORS SINCE 1916.

892 THE SWIMMING POOL ON THE TITANIC IS TECHNICALLY STILL FULL OF WATER.

893 THERE IS A SECRET ROOM HIDDEN BEHIND ABRAHAM LINCOLN'S HEAD ON MOUNT RUSHMORE.

894 NAPOLEON BONAPARTE WAS NOT SHORT; HE WAS ACTUALLY TALLER THAN THE AVERAGE FRENCHMAN OF HIS TIME.

895 ALBERT EINSTEIN HATED WEARING SOCKS AND USUALLY WENT WITHOUT THEM.

896 ALBERT EINSTEIN WAS NOT BAD AT MATH IN SCHOOL; HE HAD MASTERED CALCULUS BY AGE 15.

897 ALBERT EINSTEIN WAS OFFERED THE PRESIDENCY OF ISRAEL IN 1952, BUT HE DECLINED.

898 ANNE FRANK AND MARTIN LUTHER KING JR. WERE BORN IN THE SAME YEAR (1929).

899 HARVARD UNIVERSITY WAS FOUNDED BEFORE CALCULUS WAS EVEN DISCOVERED.

---

900 THE LAST EXECUTION BY GUILLOTINE IN FRANCE HAPPENED THE SAME YEAR STAR WARS WAS RELEASED (1977).

---

901 DURING WORLD WAR II, THE OSCARS STATUES WERE MADE OF PAINTED PLASTER BECAUSE OF A METAL SHORTAGE.

---

902 ELVIS PRESLEY'S NATURAL HAIR COLOR WAS BLONDE; HE DYED IT BLACK.

---

903 CHARLIE CHAPLIN ONCE ENTERED A "CHARLIE CHAPLIN LOOK-ALIKE CONTEST" AND CAME IN 20TH PLACE.

---

904 THE PAINT ON THE EIFFEL TOWER WEIGHS AS MUCH AS 10 ELEPHANTS.

---

905 THE FLAG OF FRANCE WAS ONCE JUST A PLAIN WHITE CLOTH (FROM 1814 TO 1830).

---

906 THE FLAG OF MOZAMBIQUE FEATURES AN IMAGE OF A MODERN AK-47 ASSAULT RIFLE.

---

907 ETHIOPIA FOLLOWS A CALENDAR THAT IS ROUGHLY SEVEN YEARS BEHIND THE REST OF THE WORLD.

908 IN ANCIENT ROME, PEOPLE USED TO WASH THEIR CLOTHES IN PEE BECAUSE THE AMMONIA NATURALLY ACTED AS A BLEACHING AGENT.

---

909 THE GREAT PYRAMID OF GIZA WAS ORIGINALLY COVERED IN HIGHLY POLISHED WHITE LIMESTONE THAT GLEAMED IN THE SUN.

---

910 JULIUS CAESAR WAS ONCE KIDNAPPED BY PIRATES AND DEMANDED THEY ASK FOR A HIGHER RANSOM BECAUSE HE THOUGHT HE WAS WORTH MORE.

---

911 THE ANCIENT CITY OF TROY, MADE FAMOUS BY THE TROJAN HORSE STORY, WAS REAL AND ITS RUINS ARE IN MODERN-DAY TURKEY.

---

912 ANCIENT EGYPTIANS BELIEVED THAT CATS WERE MAGICAL CREATURES CAPABLE OF BRINGING GOOD LUCK.

---

913 THE MAYAN CIVILIZATION USED COCOA BEANS AS A FORM OF CURRENCY TO BUY GOODS AND PAY TAXES.

---

914 ALEXANDER THE GREAT NEVER LOST A SINGLE BATTLE IN HIS 15 YEARS OF MILITARY CONQUEST.

---

915 THE EARLIEST KNOWN WRITTEN LAWS ARE THE CODE OF HAMMURABI, DATING BACK TO 1754 BC.

---

916 GLADIATORS IN ANCIENT ROME WERE SOMETIMES CONSIDERED CELEBRITIES AND EVEN ENDORSED PRODUCTS.

917 THE ANCIENT CITY OF PETRA WAS CARVED ENTIRELY OUT OF RED SANDSTONE CLIFFS.

---

918 CLEOPATRA WAS ACTUALLY GREEK, NOT EGYPTIAN, AS SHE WAS A DESCENDANT OF ONE OF ALEXANDER THE GREAT'S GENERALS.

---

919 THE LIBRARY OF ALEXANDRIA WAS ONE OF THE LARGEST LIBRARIES IN THE ANCIENT WORLD BEFORE IT TRAGICALLY BURNED DOWN.

---

920 THE TERRACOTTA ARMY IN CHINA CONTAINS OVER 8,000 UNIQUE CLAY SOLDIERS BURIED TO PROTECT THE EMPEROR IN THE AFTERLIFE.

---

921 THE ANCIENT GREEKS USED A PRIMITIVE VERSION OF A VENDING MACHINE TO DISPENSE HOLY WATER IN TEMPLES.

---

922 ANCIENT EGYPTIANS USED CARVED SLABS OF SOLID STONE AS PILLOWS.

---

923 THE ANCIENT CITY OF MOHENJO-DARO IN THE INDUS VALLEY HAD A COMPLEX INDOOR PLUMBING AND SEWAGE SYSTEM OVER 4,000 YEARS AGO.

---

924 IN ANCIENT EGYPT, BOTH MEN AND WOMEN WORE HEAVY EYE MAKEUP MADE FROM GROUND-UP MINERALS LIKE LEAD AND COPPER.

---

925 GENGHIS KHAN ESTABLISHED ONE OF THE WORLD'S FIRST INTERNATIONAL POSTAL SYSTEMS, CALLED THE YAM.

926 THE ANCIENT OLYMPICS FEATURED A SPORT CALLED PANKRATION, A BRUTAL MIX OF BOXING AND WRESTLING WITH ALMOST NO RULES.

---

927 JULIUS CAESAR WAS STABBED 23 TIMES DURING HIS ASSASSINATION, BUT ONLY ONE OF THE WOUNDS WAS ACTUALLY FATAL.

---

928 DURING THE VICTORIAN ERA, IT WAS A COMMON MOURNING TRADITION TO PHOTOGRAPH DEAD RELATIVES POSED AS IF THEY WERE STILL ALIVE.

---

929 THE ROMAN EMPIRE BUILT A VAST NETWORK OF CONCRETE ROADS, AND SOME ARE STILL IN USE TODAY.

---

930 THE FAMOUS "KEEP CALM AND CARRY ON" POSTER WAS PRINTED BY THE BRITISH GOVERNMENT DURING WWII BUT WAS RARELY SEEN BY THE PUBLIC UNTIL THE YEAR 2000.

---

931 ANCIENT MAYA DENTISTS DRILLED HOLES INTO PEOPLE'S TEETH AND EMBEDDED PRECIOUS STONES LIKE JADE AND TURQUOISE FOR DECORATION.

---

932 IN THE 18TH CENTURY, WEALTHY BRITISH LANDOWNERS WOULD HIRE "ORNAMENTAL HERMITS" TO LIVE IN CAVES IN THEIR GARDENS FOR ENTERTAINMENT.

---

933 THE GREAT FIRE OF LONDON IN 1666 DESTROYED A MASSIVE PORTION OF THE CITY, BUT THE OFFICIALLY RECORDED DEATH TOLL WAS ONLY SIX PEOPLE.

---

934 WOMEN IN ANCIENT ROME SOMETIMES DYED THEIR HAIR BLONDE USING A MIXTURE THAT INCLUDED PIGEON POOP.

935 IN 390 BC, A FLOCK OF NOISY, HONKING GEESE SAVED ROME FROM A SURPRISE NIGHT ATTACK BY WAKING UP THE GUARDS.

---

936 THE LEGENDARY HANGING GARDENS OF BABYLON MIGHT NEVER HAVE ACTUALLY EXISTED, AS NO ARCHAEOLOGICAL EVIDENCE HAS EVER BEEN FOUND.

---

937 SPARTACUS WAS A REAL THRACIAN GLADIATOR WHO LED A MASSIVE, MULTI-YEAR SLAVE UPRISING AGAINST THE ROMAN REPUBLIC.

---

938 DURING THE MIDDLE AGES, ANIMALS (LIKE PIGS AND BUGS) COULD BE OFFICIALLY PUT ON TRIAL AND EXECUTED FOR COMMITTING CRIMES.

---

939 THE LEANING TOWER OF PISA ACTUALLY STARTED LEANING WHILE IT WAS STILL BEING BUILT IN THE 12TH CENTURY DUE TO SOFT GROUND.

---

940 AZTEC WARRIORS WORE ARMOR MADE OF TIGHTLY WOVEN COTTON SOAKED IN SALTWATER, WHICH CRYSTALLIZED AND MADE IT TOUGH ENOUGH TO STOP ARROWS.

---

941 WINSTON CHURCHILL WAS KNOWN TO DRINK A WATERED-DOWN GLASS OF WHISKEY WITH HIS BREAKFAST.

---

942 THE ANCIENT OLYMPIC GAMES WERE BANNED IN 393 AD BY A ROMAN EMPEROR AND DIDN'T RETURN FOR OVER 1,500 YEARS.

---

943 DURING THE COLD WAR, THE CIA CONSIDERED DROPPING OVERSIZED CONDOMS LABELED "MEDIUM" OVER THE SOVIET UNION TO DEMORALIZE THEIR TROOPS.

944 QUEEN VICTORIA SURVIVED AT LEAST SEVEN DIFFERENT ASSASSINATION ATTEMPTS DURING HER REIGN.

---

945 THE ANCIENT PERSIANS USED A RUDIMENTARY FORM OF AIR CONDITIONING CALLED "WINDCATCHERS" TO KEEP THEIR DESERT BUILDINGS COOL.

---

946 THE SHORTEST-SERVING US PRESIDENT, WILLIAM HENRY HARRISON, DIED JUST 32 DAYS AFTER TAKING OFFICE.

FOOD & DRINK

CHAPTER 8

947 BANANAS ARE TECHNICALLY BERRIES, BUT STRAWBERRIES ARE NOT.

---

948 THE FIRST ORANGES WEREN'T ORANGE; THEY WERE ACTUALLY GREEN.

---

949 COTTON CANDY WAS INVENTED BY A DENTIST.

---

950 BROCCOLI CONTAINS MORE PROTEIN PER CALORIE THAN STEAK.

---

951 APPLES FLOAT IN WATER BECAUSE THEY ARE 25% AIR.

---

952 ARCHAEOLOGISTS HAVE FOUND POTS OF HONEY IN ANCIENT EGYPTIAN TOMBS THAT ARE STILL GOOD TO EAT.

---

953 THE FEAR OF GETTING PEANUT BUTTER STUCK ON THE ROOF OF YOUR MOUTH IS CALLED ARACHIBUTYROPHOBIA.

---

954 GUMMY BEARS ARE CALLED JELLY BABIES IN ENGLAND.

---

955 CHOCOLATE-COVERED ANTS ARE CONSIDERED A TREAT IN MEXICO.

956 WHILE A DOZEN IS 12, A BAKER'S DOZEN IS 13.

957 MILITARY SURVIVAL GUIDES INCLUDE INSTRUCTIONS TO EAT INSECTS IF NO OTHER FOOD IS AVAILABLE.

958 GRAPES ARE THE MOST POPULAR FRUIT IN THE WORLD.

959 PEOPLE ON THE EAST COAST OF THE UNITED STATES TEND TO PREFER CREAMY PEANUT BUTTER, WHILE THOSE ON THE WEST COAST PREFER CRUNCHY.

960 FRENCH FRIES WERE INVENTED IN BELGIUM.

961 A STRAND OF SPAGHETTI IS CALLED A SPAGHETTO.

962 CUCUMBERS ARE MADE UP OF 96 PERCENT WATER.

963 EATING TOO MANY CARROTS CAN TURN YOUR SKIN ORANGE.

964 THE BLUE IN BLUE CHEESE IS ACTUALLY MOLD.

965 DARKER-COLORED POPSICLES TEND TO MELT FASTER THAN LIGHTER-COLORED ONES.

---

966 THE GHOST PEPPER IS SO HOT THAT IT CAN BURN YOUR SKIN.

---

967 PERU HAS MORE THAN 3,000 DIFFERENT KINDS OF POTATOES.

---

968 PINEAPPLES TAKE TWO YEARS TO GROW.

---

969 BUBBLEGUM WAS ORIGINALLY GRAY. THE PINK COLOR WAS ADDED LATER.

---

970 MCDONALD'S ONCE DEVELOPED BUBBLEGUM-FLAVORED BROCCOLI TO GET KIDS TO EAT HEALTHIER.

---

971 IN THE 1830S, KETCHUP WAS SOLD AS MEDICINE TO CURE INDIGESTION.

---

972 THE FEAR OF VEGETABLES IS CALLED LACHANOPHOBIA.

---

973 PEANUTS ARE NOT NUTS; THEY ARE LEGUMES, LIKE PEAS AND BEANS.

974 PEANUTS CAN BE USED AS AN INGREDIENT IN MAKING DYNAMITE.

---

975 RIPE CRANBERRIES WILL BOUNCE LIKE RUBBER BALLS IF YOU DROP THEM.

---

976 APPLES, PEARS, AND CHERRIES ARE ALL BIOLOGICALLY PART OF THE ROSE FAMILY.

---

977 BANANAS ARE SLIGHTLY RADIOACTIVE BECAUSE THEY CONTAIN HIGH LEVELS OF POTASSIUM.

---

978 POTATO CHIPS WERE INVENTED BY A CHEF WHO WAS TRYING TO ANNOY A CUSTOMER WHO COMPLAINED HIS FRIES WERE TOO THICK.

---

979 A "POUND CAKE" GOT ITS NAME BECAUSE THE ORIGINAL RECIPE USED ONE POUND OF EVERY INGREDIENT.

---

980 THE SANDWICH IS NAMED AFTER THE EARL OF SANDWICH, WHO WANTED FOOD HE COULD EAT WITHOUT STOPPING HIS CARD GAME.

---

981 CROISSANTS WERE ORIGINALLY CREATED IN AUSTRIA, NOT FRANCE.

---

982 LEMONS WILL FLOAT IN A BUCKET OF WATER, BUT LIMES WILL SINK.

983 STRAWBERRIES ARE THE ONLY FRUIT THAT HAVE THEIR SEEDS ON THE OUTSIDE.

---

984 CARROTS WERE ORIGINALLY PURPLE, NOT ORANGE.

---

986 WHITE CHOCOLATE IS NOT TECHNICALLY CHOCOLATE BECAUSE IT CONTAINS NO COCOA SOLIDS.

---

986 ALL COLORS OF FROOT LOOPS CEREAL TASTE EXACTLY THE SAME.

---

987 PINEAPPLES CONTAIN AN ENZYME THAT DIGESTS PROTEIN, WHICH IS WHY YOUR TONGUE MIGHT TINGLE WHEN YOU EAT THEM.

---

988 FRESH EGGS SINK IN WATER, BUT BAD EGGS FLOAT BECAUSE GAS BUILDS UP INSIDE THEM.

---

989 APPLES ARE MORE EFFECTIVE AT WAKING YOU UP IN THE MORNING THAN COFFEE.

---

990 CHOCOLATE WAS ONCE USED AS MONEY BY THE ANCIENT AZTECS AND MAYANS.

---

991 MOST OF THE VITAMIN C IN A POTATO IS FOUND IN THE SKIN.

992 A JAR OF NUTELLA IS SOLD EVERY 2.5 SECONDS.

993 CAP'N CRUNCH'S FULL NAME IS HORATIO MAGELLAN CRUNCH.

994 COOKIE MONSTER'S REAL NAME IS SID.

995 COTTON CANDY WAS ORIGINALLY CALLED "FAIRY FLOSS".

996 GERMAN CHOCOLATE CAKE IS NAMED AFTER A MAN NAMED SAM GERMAN, NOT THE COUNTRY.

997 HAWAIIAN PIZZA WAS INVENTED IN CANADA.

998 BANANAS ARE CURVED BECAUSE THEY GROW TOWARDS THE SUN.

999 A PUMPKIN IS TECHNICALLY A FRUIT.

1000 CASHEWS GROW ON THE BOTTOM OF A FRUIT CALLED A CASHEW APPLE.

1001 MCDONALD'S SELLS ABOUT 75 HAMBURGERS EVERY SINGLE SECOND.

1002 NUTELLA WAS INVENTED DURING WWII BECAUSE COCOA WAS SCARCE.

1003 RED BELL PEPPERS HAVE MORE VITAMIN C THAN ORANGES.

1004 FORTUNE COOKIES WERE ACTUALLY INVENTED IN SAN FRANCISCO, NOT CHINA.

1005 MOST "WASABI" SOLD IN STORES IS JUST COLORED HORSERADISH.

1006 THE NAME SPAM STANDS FOR "SPICED HAM".

1007 MUSHROOMS ARE BIOLOGICALLY CLOSER TO HUMANS THAN THEY ARE TO PLANTS.

1008 A WATERMELON IS MADE UP OF 92% WATER.

1009 KETCHUP LEAVES THE GLASS BOTTLE AT A SPEED OF 0.028 MILES PER HOUR.

1010 IF YOU PUT A GRAPE IN THE MICROWAVE, IT CAN CREATE A TINY EXPLOSION OF PLASMA.

1011 ALMONDS ARE MEMBERS OF THE PEACH FAMILY.

1012 CAESAR SALAD WAS INVENTED IN MEXICO, NOT ITALY.

1013 APPLE PIE ORIGINATED IN ENGLAND, NOT AMERICA.

1014 RED FOOD DYE IS OFTEN MADE FROM CRUSHED BUGS CALLED COCHINEAL.

1015 FIGS ARE POLLINATED BY WASPS THAT SOMETIMES GET TRAPPED INSIDE THE FRUIT.

1016 CASHEWS ARE IN THE SAME PLANT FAMILY AS POISON IVY.

1017 CORN EARS ALWAYS HAVE AN EVEN NUMBER OF ROWS.

1018 RHUBARB LEAVES ARE POISONOUS TO EAT.

1019 CHOCOLATE CHIP COOKIES WERE INVENTED BY ACCIDENT WHEN THE CHOCOLATE DIDN'T MELT.

1020 COCA-COLA WAS ORIGINALLY INVENTED AS A MEDICINE FOR HEADACHES.

1021 THE THREE DOTS IN THE DOMINO'S PIZZA LOGO REPRESENT THE FIRST THREE STORES THEY OPENED.

1022 HAAGEN-DAZS IS A MADE-UP WORD THAT MEANS ABSOLUTELY NOTHING.

1023 THE AVERAGE PERSON WILL EAT ABOUT 35 TONS OF FOOD IN THEIR LIFETIME.

1024 PISTACHIOS ARE ACTUALLY FRUITS, AND THEY CAN SPONTANEOUSLY COMBUST IF STORED IN LARGE, OILY PILES.

1025 TEA BAGS WERE INVENTED BY ACCIDENT WHEN CUSTOMERS THOUGHT THEY WERE SUPPOSED TO DUNK THE SAMPLE BAGS IN WATER.

1026 WAFFLE CONES WERE INVENTED AT THE WORLD'S FAIR WHEN AN ICE CREAM VENDOR RAN OUT OF BOWLS.

1027 MOUNTAIN DEW WAS ORIGINALLY CREATED TO BE MIXED WITH WHISKEY.

1028 PEANUT BUTTER CAN BE TURNED INTO DIAMONDS IF YOU SUBJECT IT TO EXTREMELY HIGH PRESSURE.

1029 BROWN SUGAR IS JUST WHITE SUGAR MIXED WITH MOLASSES.

1030 TACO BELL IS NAMED AFTER ITS FOUNDER, GLEN BELL.

1031 WENDY'S IS NAMED AFTER THE FOUNDER'S DAUGHTER.

1032 PEZ CANDY WAS ORIGINALLY INVENTED AS A BREATH MINT FOR SMOKERS.

1033 7-UP ORIGINALLY CONTAINED LITHIUM, A CHEMICAL USED TO TREAT MOOD SWINGS.

1034 THOMAS JEFFERSON IS CREDITED WITH POPULARIZING MACARONI AND CHEESE IN THE UNITED STATES AFTER TRYING IT IN FRANCE.

1035 BEN & JERRY LEARNED HOW TO MAKE ICE CREAM BY TAKING A $5 CORRESPONDENCE COURSE FROM PENN STATE.

1036 THE SHAPE OF A TOBLERONE CHOCOLATE BAR IS BASED ON THE MATTERHORN MOUNTAIN IN THE SWISS ALPS.

1037 MCDONALD'S CHICKEN MCNUGGETS COME IN FOUR SPECIFIC SHAPES: THE BOOT, THE BALL, THE BONE, AND THE BELL.

1038 THE FILLING INSIDE A KIT KAT BAR IS ACTUALLY MADE OF CRUSHED-UP KIT KATS THAT WERE BROKEN DURING PRODUCTION.

1039 BANANAS ARE GENETICALLY ALMOST IDENTICAL TO EACH OTHER BECAUSE THEY ARE CLONES.

1040 THE MYTH THAT CARROTS HELP YOU SEE IN THE DARK WAS WORLD WAR II PROPAGANDA INVENTED BY THE BRITISH TO HIDE THEIR RADAR TECHNOLOGY.

1041 CRANBERRIES ARE SOMETIMES CALLED "BOUNCE BERRIES" BECAUSE RIPE ONES BOUNCE WHEN YOU DROP THEM.

1042 FANTA WAS INVENTED IN GERMANY DURING WORLD WAR II BECAUSE THEY COULDN'T GET THE SYRUP TO MAKE COCA-COLA.

1043 THE COLOR "ORANGE" WAS NAMED AFTER THE FRUIT, NOT THE OTHER WAY AROUND.

1044 THERE IS A TROPICAL FRUIT CALLED THE "BLACK SAPOTE" THAT NATURALLY TASTES EXACTLY LIKE CHOCOLATE PUDDING.

1045 THE WORLD'S LONGEST INDIVIDUAL FRENCH FRY EVER FOUND MEASURED 34 INCHES LONG.

1046 THE INVENTOR OF THE CHOCOLATE CHIP COOKIE SOLD HER FAMOUS RECIPE TO NESTLÉ IN EXCHANGE FOR A LIFETIME SUPPLY OF CHOCOLATE.

1047 HONEY IS THE ONLY FOOD THAT INCLUDES ALL THE SUBSTANCES NECESSARY TO SUSTAIN LIFE, INCLUDING ENZYMES, VITAMINS, MINERALS, AND WATER.

1048 APPLESAUCE WAS THE FIRST FOOD EATEN BY AN AMERICAN ASTRONAUT IN SPACE.

1049 THE MOST EXPENSIVE PIZZA EVER CREATED COST $12,000 AND TOOK 72 HOURS TO MAKE.

1050 FRITOS WERE INVENTED BY A MAN WHO BOUGHT THE RECIPE FOR $100 FROM A CAFE OWNER.

1051 MACADAMIA NUTS ARE EXTREMELY TOXIC TO DOGS, EVEN IN SMALL AMOUNTS.

1052 THE FEAR OF COOKING IS CALLED MAGEIROCOPHOBIA.

1053 WATERMELONS ARE BOTH A FRUIT AND A VEGETABLE BECAUSE THEY ARE PART OF THE GOURD FAMILY.

1054 REAL VANILLA EXTRACT COMES FROM THE SEED POD OF A SPECIFIC TYPE OF ORCHID FLOWER.

1055 THE LARGEST PIZZA EVER MADE WAS OVER 13,000 SQUARE FEET AND WAS MADE IN ROME.

1056 A SINGLE STRAWBERRY HAS ABOUT 200 TINY SEEDS ON ITS OUTSIDE.

1057 A CLUSTER OF BANANAS IS OFFICIALLY CALLED A "HAND", AND A SINGLE BANANA IS A "FINGER".

1058 SAFFRON IS THE MOST EXPENSIVE SPICE IN THE WORLD BECAUSE EVERY FLOWER THREAD MUST BE CAREFULLY PICKED BY HAND.

1059 POUND FOR POUND, THERE IS MORE SUGAR IN A LEMON THAN THERE IS IN A STRAWBERRY.

1060 PEACHES AND NECTARINES ARE THE EXACT SAME FRUIT, SEPARATED BY JUST ONE GENE THAT GIVES PEACHES THEIR FUZZ.

1061 THE SIGNATURE HOLES IN SWISS CHEESE ARE ACTUALLY CARBON DIOXIDE GAS BUBBLES RELEASED BY BACTERIA.

1062 TONIC WATER GLOWS BRIGHT BLUE UNDER A BLACKLIGHT BECAUSE IT CONTAINS A FLUORESCENT COMPOUND CALLED QUININE.

1063 KETCHUP WAS ORIGINALLY A FERMENTED FISH SAUCE FROM ANCIENT CHINA, WITH NO TOMATOES INVOLVED.

1064 "BABY CARROTS" DO NOT GROW THAT WAY; THEY ARE SIMPLY UGLY OR BROKEN ADULT CARROTS WHITTLED DOWN BY A MACHINE.

1065 THE EXPIRATION DATE ON A PLASTIC BOTTLE OF WATER IS ACTUALLY FOR THE PLASTIC BOTTLE ITSELF, NOT THE WATER INSIDE.

1066 CORN IS GROWN ON EVERY SINGLE CONTINENT ON EARTH EXCEPT FOR ANTARCTICA.

1067 THE SPICES CILANTRO AND CORIANDER COME FROM DIFFERENT PARTS OF THE EXACT SAME PLANT.

1068 BLACK PEPPER WAS ONCE SO VALUABLE DURING THE MIDDLE AGES THAT IT WAS USED AS CURRENCY TO PAY RENT.

1069 IT TAKES ROUGHLY 540 PEANUTS TO MAKE A STANDARD 12-OUNCE JAR OF PEANUT BUTTER.

1070 GELATIN, THE MAIN INGREDIENT IN JELL-O, IS MADE BY BOILING THE BONES AND CONNECTIVE TISSUES OF ANIMALS.

1071 AVOCADOS WERE ORIGINALLY CALLED "ALLIGATOR PEARS" WHEN THEY WERE FIRST INTRODUCED TO THE ENGLISH-SPEAKING WORLD.

1072 IN JAPAN, CHEFS MUST TRAIN FOR SEVERAL YEARS TO GET A SPECIAL LICENSE TO SAFELY PREPARE DEADLY PUFFERFISH.

1073 DECAFFEINATED COFFEE IS NOT 100% CAFFEINE-FREE; A STANDARD CUP STILL CONTAINS TRACE AMOUNTS.

1074 OYSTERS ARE TYPICALLY STILL ALIVE RIGHT UP UNTIL THE MOMENT YOU SWALLOW THEM RAW.

1075 CILANTRO TASTES LIKE SOAP TO ABOUT 10% OF THE POPULATION DUE TO A HARMLESS GENETIC MUTATION.

1076 THE WORD "CANOLA" IN CANOLA OIL IS A MADE-UP ABBREVIATION THAT STANDS FOR "CANADIAN OIL, LOW ACID".

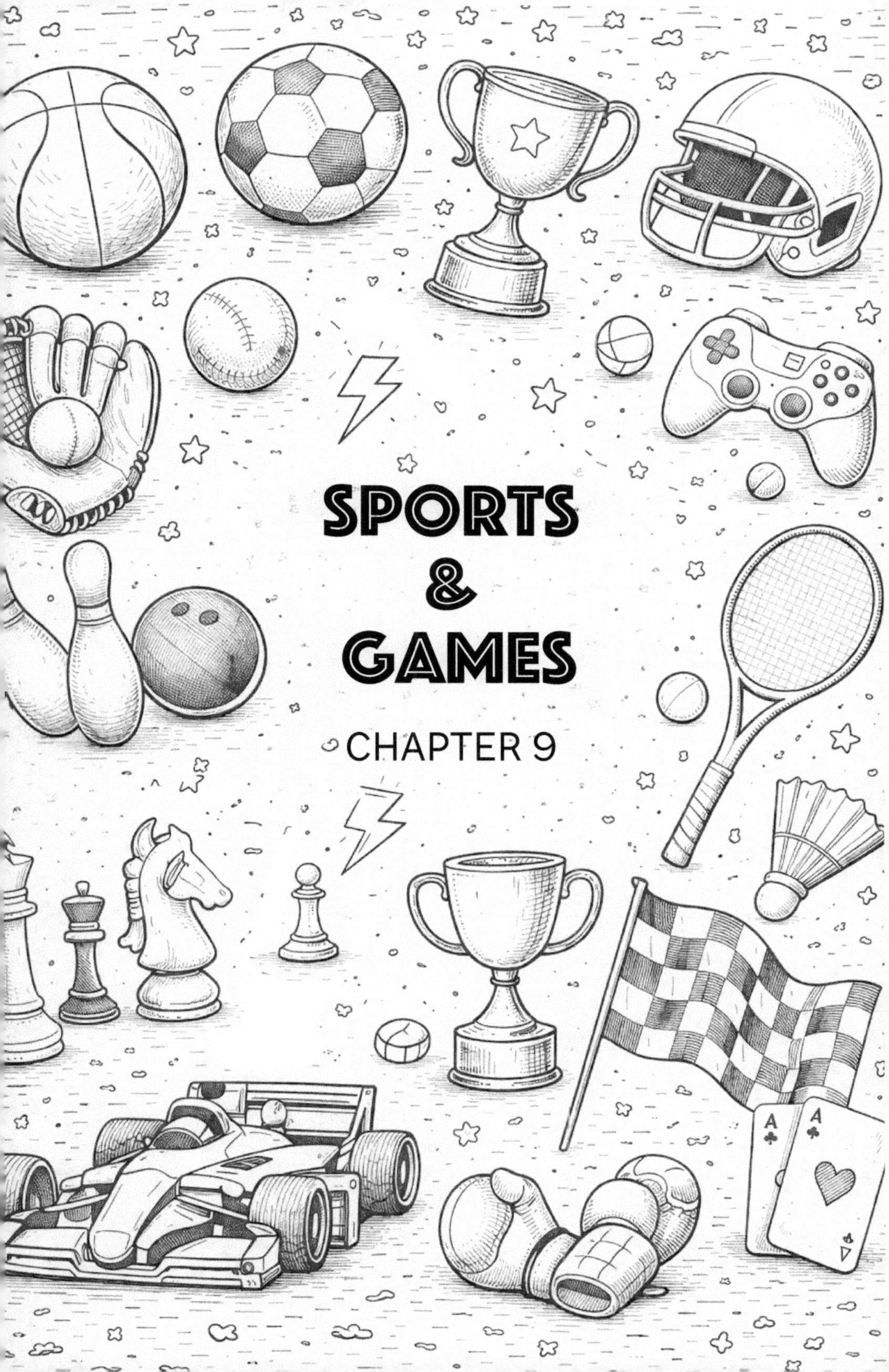
SPORTS
&
GAMES
CHAPTER 9

1077 IN NASCAR RACES, FOUR TIRES ARE CHANGED AND THE CAR IS REFUELED IN FEWER THAN 15 SECONDS.

1078 THE BOARD GAME MANCALA ORIGINATED IN ANCIENT AFRICA.

1079 EARLY OLYMPIC ATHLETES IN ANCIENT GREECE COMPETED NAKED.

1080 IN BOWLING, THREE STRIKES IN A ROW IS CALLED A TURKEY.

1081 LEGO BRICKS WERE ORIGINALLY CREATED IN DENMARK.

1082 A DUEL BETWEEN THREE PEOPLE IS CALLED A TRUEL.

1083 BASKETBALL WAS ORIGINALLY PLAYED USING A SOCCER BALL AND PEACH BASKETS.

1084 GOLF IS THE ONLY SPORT THAT HAS EVER BEEN PLAYED ON THE MOON.

1085 OLYMPIC GOLD MEDALS ARE NOT MADE OF GOLD; THEY ARE MOSTLY SILVER.

1086 THERE ARE MORE THAN 43 QUINTILLION POSSIBLE WAYS TO SCRAMBLE A RUBIK'S CUBE.

1087 BARBIE'S FULL REAL NAME IS BARBARA MILLICENT ROBERTS.

1088 THE LONGEST TENNIS MATCH IN HISTORY LASTED 11 HOURS AND 5 MINUTES.

1089 TENNIS WAS ORIGINALLY PLAYED WITH BARE HANDS; RACKETS WERE ADDED LATER.

1090 THE OLYMPIC RINGS FEATURE FIVE COLORS (BLUE, YELLOW, BLACK, GREEN, AND RED) BECAUSE EVERY COUNTRY'S FLAG CONTAINS AT LEAST ONE OF THEM.

1091 GOLF BALLS HAVE DIMPLES BECAUSE THEY HELP THE BALL FLY FARTHER.

1092 IF YOU SHUFFLE A DECK OF CARDS EFFECTIVELY, IT IS MATHEMATICALLY LIKELY THAT THE EXACT ORDER OF CARDS HAS NEVER EXISTED BEFORE IN THE HISTORY OF THE UNIVERSE.

1093 THERE IS A SECRET BASKETBALL COURT INSIDE THE MATTERHORN RIDE AT DISNEYLAND.

1094 NINTENDO'S MARIO WAS ORIGINALLY NAMED "JUMPMAN" BEFORE HIS NAME WAS CHANGED.

1095 SONIC THE HEDGEHOG WAS ORIGINALLY GOING TO BE A RABBIT BEFORE THEY DECIDED ON A HEDGEHOG.

1096 THE FOUR-BLOCK SHAPES IN THE GAME TETRIS ARE OFFICIALLY CALLED "TETROMINOES".

1097 IN THE ORIGINAL PAC-MAN GAME, THE GHOSTS HAD SPECIFIC PERSONALITIES: ONE CHASES, ONE AMBUSHES, ONE IS RANDOM, AND ONE MIMICS YOU.

1098 TUG-OF-WAR USED TO BE AN OLYMPIC SPORT.

1099 PAINTING USED TO BE AN OLYMPIC SPORT.

1100 MICHAEL JORDAN WAS CUT FROM HIS HIGH SCHOOL BASKETBALL TEAM.

1101 A REGULATION GOLF BALL HAS 336 DIMPLES.

1102 A STANDARD SOCCER BALL IS MADE OF 32 PANELS, REPRESENTING THE COUNTRIES IN EUROPE AND SOUTH AMERICA.

1103 VOLLEYBALL WAS INVENTED AS A MIXTURE OF BASKETBALL, BASEBALL, TENNIS, AND HANDBALL.

1104 THE SUPER BOWL TROPHY IS MADE BY TIFFANY & CO. AND COSTS $50,000 TO PRODUCE.

1105 THERE IS A BASKETBALL COURT ON THE TOP FLOOR OF THE U.S. SUPREME COURT BUILDING (KNOWN AS THE “HIGHEST COURT IN THE LAND”).

1106 GOLF BALLS WERE ORIGINALLY MADE OF LEATHER STUFFED WITH FEATHERS.

1107 THERE ARE MORE POSSIBLE GAMES OF CHESS THAN THERE ARE ATOMS IN THE KNOWN UNIVERSE.

1108 FRISBEES WERE ORIGINALLY METAL PIE TINS THROWN BY COLLEGE STUDENTS.

1109 TABLE TENNIS WAS ORIGINALLY CALLED “WHIFF-WHAFF”.

1110 BABE RUTH USED TO KEEP A WET CABBAGE LEAF UNDER HIS HAT TO KEEP COOL DURING GAMES.

1111 THE GRASS AT WIMBLEDON IS TRIMMED TO EXACTLY 8MM TALL.

1112 THERE ARE MORE LEGO MINIFIGURES IN THE WORLD THAN THERE ARE PEOPLE.

1113 BARBIE HAS HAD OVER 200 DIFFERENT CAREERS, FROM ASTRONAUT TO PRESIDENT.

1114 THE FIRST TOY EVER ADVERTISED ON TV WAS MR. POTATO HEAD IN 1952.

1115 THE INVENTOR OF THE FRISBEE WAS TURNED INTO A FRISBEE AFTER HE DIED (HIS ASHES WERE MOLDED INTO ONE).

1116 THE RUBIK'S CUBE WAS INVENTED BY A PROFESSOR TO HELP HIS STUDENTS UNDERSTAND 3D GEOMETRY.

1117 THE SLINKY WAS INDUCTED INTO THE TOY HALL OF FAME.

1118 PLAY-DOH WAS ORIGINALLY WHITE; THEY ADDED COLORS LATER WHEN IT BECAME A TOY.

1119 IF YOU LOOK CLOSELY AT SUPER MARIO, HE HITS THE BLOCKS WITH HIS FIST, NOT HIS HEAD.

1120 THE WORD "POKÉMON" IS A CONTRACTION OF THE JAPANESE WORDS FOR "POCKET MONSTERS".

1121 THE VERY FIRST POKÉMON EVER DESIGNED WAS NOT PIKACHU, BUT RHYDON.

1122 PIKACHU'S NAME COMES FROM THE JAPANESE SOUNDS FOR SPARKLING ("PIKA") AND SQUEAKING ("CHU").

1123 THE "CREEPER" IN MINECRAFT WAS CREATED BY ACCIDENT WHEN THE DEVELOPER TRIED TO MAKE A PIG BUT MESSED UP THE CODE FOR THE SHAPE.

1124 THE GAME ROBLOX WAS ORIGINALLY GOING TO BE CALLED "DYNABLOCKS".

1125 IN THE GAME AMONG US, THE "SHHH" SOUND AT THE START IS A RECORDING OF ONE OF THE DEVELOPERS SHUSHING THEIR MICROPHONE.

1126 THE VIDEO GAME FORTNITE MADE MORE MONEY IN ITS FIRST TWO YEARS THAN THE HIGHEST-GROSSING MOVIE IN HISTORY.

1127 A STANDARD DECK OF CARDS REPRESENTS A CALENDAR: 4 SUITS FOR THE SEASONS, 12 FACE CARDS FOR THE MONTHS, AND 52 CARDS FOR THE WEEKS.

1128 THE SPOTS ON A DIE ARE OFFICIALLY CALLED "PIPS".

1129 THE OPPOSITE SIDES OF A STANDARD DIE ALWAYS ADD UP TO THE NUMBER SEVEN.

1130 THE GAME OF CHESS ORIGINATED IN INDIA OVER 1,500 YEARS AGO.

1131 SCRABBLE WAS INVENTED BY AN ARCHITECT WHO WAS OUT OF WORK DURING THE GREAT DEPRESSION.

1132 SILLY STRING WAS ORIGINALLY INVENTED TO BE A SPRAY-ON CAST FOR BROKEN BONES.

1133 THE GAME TWISTER WAS ORIGINALLY CALLED "PRETZEL".

1134 SLINKYS WERE USED BY SOLDIERS IN THE VIETNAM WAR AS MAKESHIFT RADIO ANTENNAS.

1135 BARBIE HAS THREE SISTERS NAMED SKIPPER, STACIE, AND CHELSEA.

1136 BARBIE'S BOYFRIEND KEN HAS A LAST NAME: CARSON.

1137 HOT WHEELS CARS WERE DESIGNED BY A REAL ROCKET SCIENTIST.

1138 "NERF" STANDS FOR "NON-EXPANDING RECREATIONAL FOAM".

1139 LEGO BRICKS MADE IN 1958 WILL STILL FIT PERFECTLY WITH LEGO BRICKS MADE TODAY.

1140 IF YOU BUILT A COLUMN OF LEGO BRICKS TO REACH THE MOON, IT WOULD TAKE ABOUT 40 BILLION BRICKS.

1141 MCDONALD'S IS TECHNICALLY THE WORLD'S LARGEST TOY DISTRIBUTOR BECAUSE OF HAPPY MEALS.

1142 EVERY CABBAGE PATCH KID DOLL COMES WITH ITS OWN UNIQUE BIRTH CERTIFICATE AND NAME.

1143 THE FURBY TOY WAS BANNED FROM THE PENTAGON BECAUSE INTELLIGENCE OFFICERS THOUGHT IT MIGHT BE A SPY DEVICE.

1144 THE ETCH A SKETCH WAS INVENTED BY A MAN WHO WAS PEELING A DECAL OFF A LIGHT SWITCH AND NOTICED HOW IT TRANSFERRED.

1145 THE NAME OF THE GAME "JENGA" COMES FROM A SWAHILI WORD MEANING "TO BUILD".

1146 THE CARD GAME "UNO" IS NAMED AFTER THE SPANISH AND ITALIAN WORD FOR "ONE".

1147 A STANDARD DECK OF CARDS WEIGHS ABOUT 94 GRAMS.

1148 THE LIQUID INSIDE A MAGIC 8 BALL IS ESSENTIALLY BLUE DYE MIXED WITH ALCOHOL.

1149 THE YO-YO IS CONSIDERED THE SECOND OLDEST TOY IN HISTORY, WITH THE DOLL BEING THE OLDEST.

1150 A NINTENDO GAME BOY ONCE SURVIVED AN EXPLOSION IN A WAR AND STILL WORKED; IT IS NOW IN A MUSEUM.

1151 THE PLAYSTATION 2 IS THE BEST-SELLING VIDEO GAME CONSOLE OF ALL TIME.

1152 MARIO WAS NAMED AFTER THE LANDLORD OF THE WAREHOUSE WHERE NINTENDO OF AMERICA WAS HEADQUARTERED.

1153 THE RICH MAN IN THE MONOPOLY GAME IS NAMED MILBURN PENNYBAGS.

1154 THE PATIENT IN THE BOARD GAME OPERATION IS NAMED CAVITY SAM.

1155 "CHECKMATE" COMES FROM THE PERSIAN PHRASE "SHAH MAT," WHICH MEANS "THE KING IS HELPLESS".

1156 THE STANDARD COLOR OF A TENNIS BALL WAS CHANGED TO YELLOW IN 1972 SO IT WOULD BE MORE VISIBLE ON COLOR TV.

1157 THE KING OF HEARTS IS THE ONLY KING IN A DECK OF CARDS WITHOUT A MUSTACHE.

1158 THE LONGEST MARATHON EVER RUN TOOK A MAN OVER 54 YEARS TO OFFICIALLY COMPLETE, AS HE DROPPED OUT, WENT HOME, AND RETURNED DECADES LATER TO FINISH.

1159 CURLING STONES USED IN THE OLYMPICS ARE MADE FROM A RARE TYPE OF GRANITE FOUND ONLY ON A SINGLE ISLAND IN SCOTLAND.

1160 THE FIRST MODERN OLYMPIC GAMES IN 1896 FEATURED ONLY 9 SPORTS AND 43 EVENTS.

1161 THE GAME OF BASKETBALL WAS PLAYED WITH A BROWN BALL UNTIL THE 1950S, WHEN A COACH INTRODUCED THE ORANGE BALL SO IT WAS EASIER FOR FANS TO SEE.

1162 TABLE TENNIS BALLS CAN TRAVEL AT SPEEDS EXCEEDING 60 MILES PER HOUR DURING A PROFESSIONAL MATCH.

1163 BADMINTON WAS ORIGINALLY CALLED "POONA" WHEN IT WAS PLAYED IN INDIA IN THE 1800S.

1164 A STANDARD BASEBALL HAS EXACTLY 108 RED DOUBLE STITCHES HOLDING THE LEATHER COVER TOGETHER.

1165 THE LONGEST GOLF DRIVE EVER RECORDED WAS 515 YARDS.

1166 SURFING IS ONE OF THE OLDEST SPORTS ON EARTH, WITH ORIGINS TRACING BACK OVER A THOUSAND YEARS IN POLYNESIA.

1167 A BOWLING PIN ONLY NEEDS TO TILT 7.5 DEGREES TO FALL OVER.

1168 POLO IS KNOWN AS THE "SPORT OF KINGS" AND IS CONSIDERED THE OLDEST EQUESTRIAN SPORT.

1169 THE VERY FIRST GAME OF ICE HOCKEY USING A PUCK WAS PLAYED IN CANADA IN 1875.

1170 GYMNASTICS WAS ORIGINALLY INTRODUCED IN ANCIENT GREECE TO TRAIN SOLDIERS FOR WAR.

1171 AN OLYMPIC SWIMMING POOL HOLDS ABOUT 660,000 GALLONS OF WATER.

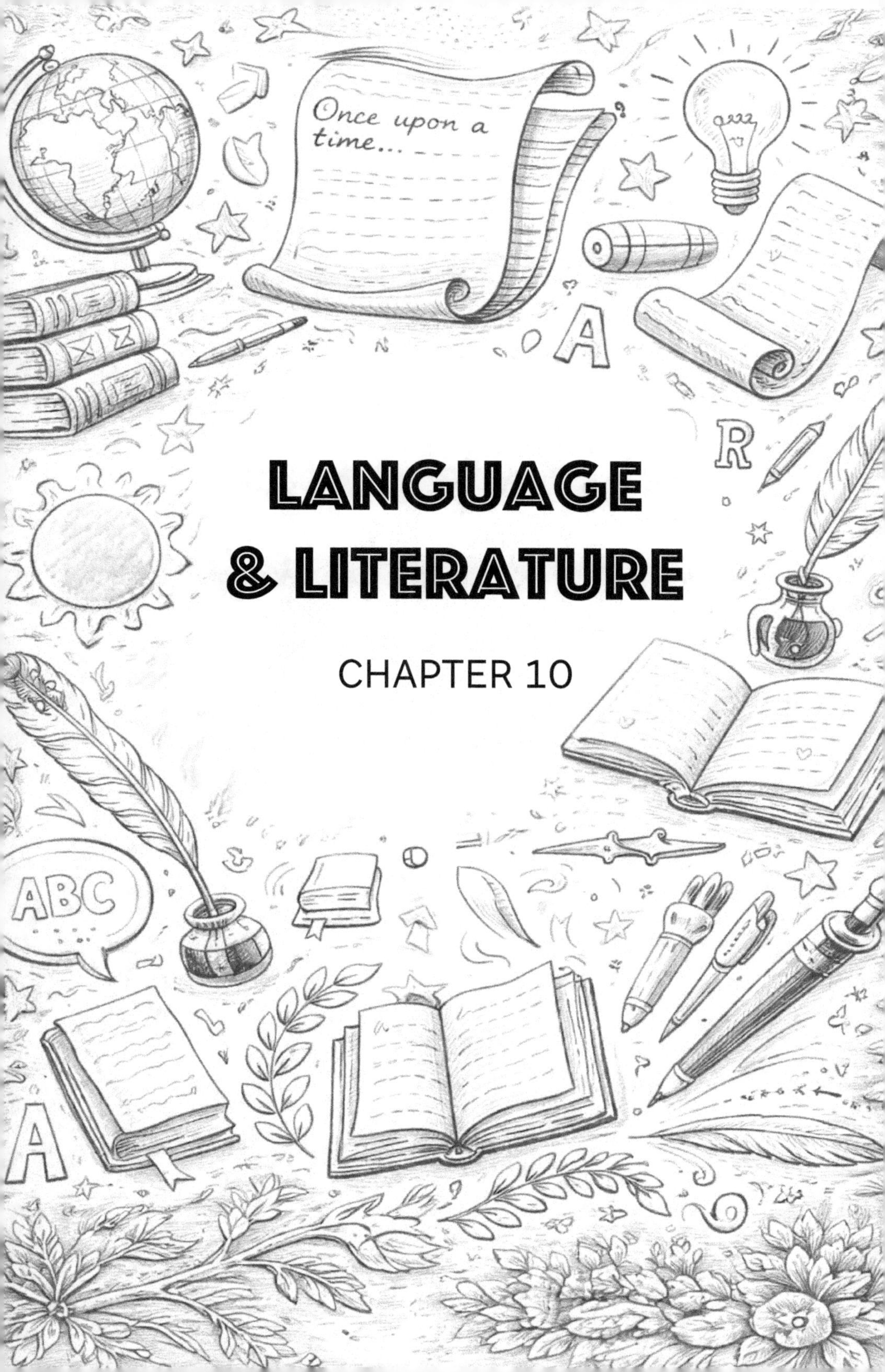

LANGUAGE & LITERATURE

CHAPTER 10

1172 THE LONGEST ENGLISH WORD IS 189,819 LETTERS LONG; IT IS THE CHEMICAL NAME FOR TITIN AND WOULD TAKE OVER THREE AND A HALF HOURS TO PRONOUNCE.

1173 THE ENGLISH NUMBER "FOUR" IS THE ONLY NUMBER SPELLED WITH THE SAME NUMBER OF LETTERS AS THE AMOUNT IT DESCRIBES.

1174 THE NAME FOR THE PLEASANT SCENT OF OLD BOOKS IS "BIBLIOSMIA".

1175 THE HAWAIIAN WORD "ALOHA" MEANS BOTH HELLO AND GOODBYE.

1176 THE BIBLE IS THE WORLD'S BEST-SELLING BOOK OF ALL TIME.

1177 HANDWRITING STARTED IN SUMERIA 5,000 YEARS AGO AS A SERIES OF INDENTATIONS IN CLAY TABLETS.

1178 EVERY NUMBER FROM 89 ON HAS THE LETTER "N" IN ITS NAME.

1179 "FORTY" IS THE ONLY NUMBER WHOSE LETTERS APPEAR IN ALPHABETICAL ORDER.

1180 MORE THAN 7,000 LANGUAGES ARE SPOKEN AROUND THE WORLD TODAY.

1181 THE "POUND" OR "HASHTAG" SYMBOL (#) ON YOUR KEYBOARD IS OFFICIALLY CALLED AN OCTOTHORPE.

1182 THE DOT OVER THE LOWERCASE LETTER "I" AND "J" IS OFFICIALLY CALLED A TITTLE.

1183 THE LETTER "Q" IS THE ONLY LETTER THAT DOES NOT APPEAR IN ANY U.S. STATE NAME.

1184 THE WORD "MUSCLE" COMES FROM A LATIN TERM MEANING "LITTLE MOUSE," BECAUSE ANCIENT ROMANS THOUGHT FLEXING MUSCLES LOOKED LIKE MICE MOVING UNDER THE SKIN.

1185 "DREAMT" IS THE ONLY COMMON WORD IN THE ENGLISH LANGUAGE THAT ENDS WITH THE LETTERS "MT".

1186 THE WORD "RHYTHM" IS THE LONGEST ENGLISH WORD WITHOUT A STANDARD VOWEL (A, E, I, O, U), THOUGH "RHYTHMS" IS SLIGHTLY LONGER.

1187 THERE ARE NO WORDS IN THE ENGLISH LANGUAGE THAT PERFECTLY RHYME WITH "ORANGE," "SILVER," OR "PURPLE".

1188 WILLIAM SHAKESPEARE INVENTED THE WORD "PUKING".

1189 THE LETTER "E" IS THE MOST COMMON LETTER USED IN THE ENGLISH LANGUAGE.

1190 THE WORD "QUEUE" IS JUST THE LETTER Q FOLLOWED BY FOUR SILENT LETTERS.

1191 "TYPEWRITER" IS THE LONGEST COMMON WORD YOU CAN TYPE USING ONLY THE TOP ROW OF A STANDARD KEYBOARD.

1192 THE WORD "BOOKKEEPER" IS THE ONLY WORD IN THE ENGLISH LANGUAGE WITH THREE DOUBLE LETTERS IN A ROW.

1193 IF YOU SPELL OUT ALL THE NUMBERS FROM ONE TO 999, YOU WILL NOT FIND THE LETTER "A" UNTIL YOU REACH ONE THOUSAND.

1194 THE PHRASE "LONG TIME NO SEE" IS ACTUALLY A DIRECT TRANSLATION OF A CHINESE IDIOM.

1195 "ALMOST" IS THE LONGEST WORD IN THE ENGLISH LANGUAGE WITH ALL OF ITS LETTERS IN ALPHABETICAL ORDER.

1196 THERE IS NO SINGLE WORD IN THE ENGLISH LANGUAGE THAT RHYMES WITH "WOLF".

1197 IRONICALLY, THE FEAR OF LONG WORDS IS CALLED HIPPOPOTOMONSTROSESQUIPPEDALIOPHOBIA.

1198 IN SCOTLAND, THERE ARE MORE THAN 400 DISTINCT WORDS FOR SNOW.

1199 THE LETTER "J" IS THE ONLY LETTER IN THE ALPHABET THAT DOES NOT APPEAR ANYWHERE ON THE PERIODIC TABLE OF ELEMENTS.

1200 "UNDERGROUND" IS THE ONLY COMMON WORD IN THE ENGLISH LANGUAGE THAT BEGINS AND ENDS WITH THE LETTERS "UND".

1201 "GO" IS THE SHORTEST COMPLETE SENTENCE IN THE ENGLISH LANGUAGE.

1202 THE WORD "SET" HAS MORE SEPARATE DEFINITIONS THAN ANY OTHER WORD IN THE DICTIONARY, TOTALING 464.

1203 DR. SEUSS WROTE "GREEN EGGS AND HAM" ON A BET THAT HE COULDN'T WRITE A BOOK USING ONLY 50 WORDS.

1204 THE AMPERSAND SYMBOL (&) WAS ONCE CONSIDERED THE 27TH LETTER OF THE ALPHABET.

1205 THE NUMBER ZERO WAS NOT INVENTED UNTIL NEARLY 1,000 YEARS AFTER OTHER NUMBERS.

1206 THE MATHEMATICAL SYMBOL FOR DIVISION (÷) IS OFFICIALLY CALLED AN OBELUS.

1207 THE HORIZONTAL LINE THAT SEPARATES THE TOP AND BOTTOM NUMBERS IN A FRACTION IS CALLED A VINCULUM.

1208 THE WORD "UNCOPYRIGHTABLE" IS ONE OF THE LONGEST ENGLISH WORDS THAT DOES NOT REPEAT A SINGLE LETTER.

1209 THE WORD "SUBDERMATOGLYPHIC" IS ANOTHER INCREDIBLY LONG ENGLISH WORD THAT DOESN'T REPEAT ANY LETTERS.

1210 THE WORD "HUNDRED" COMES FROM THE OLD NORSE WORD "HUNDRATH," WHICH ACTUALLY MEANT 120, NOT 100.

1211 "STRENGTHS" IS THE LONGEST WORD IN THE ENGLISH LANGUAGE THAT CONTAINS ONLY ONE VOWEL.

1212 THE OLDEST KNOWN "YOUR MOM" JOKE WAS DISCOVERED ON A 3,500-YEAR-OLD BABYLONIAN TABLET.

1213 "OK" STANDS FOR "OLL KORRECT," WHICH WAS A TRENDY, FUNNY MISSPELLING FROM THE 1830S.

1214 THE WORD "ROBOT" COMES FROM A CZECH WORD MEANING "FORCED LABOR".

1215 THE WORD "SALARY" COMES FROM "SALT" BECAUSE ROMAN SOLDIERS WERE FAMOUSLY PAID WITH IT.

1216 "DYSANIA" IS THE OFFICIAL TERM FOR THE FEELING OF FINDING IT HARD TO GET OUT OF BED IN THE MORNING.

1217 THE DAY AFTER TOMORROW IS TECHNICALLY CALLED "OVERMORROW".

1218 THE COMBINATION OF A QUESTION MARK AND AN EXCLAMATION POINT (?!) IS OFFICIALLY CALLED AN INTERROBANG.

1219 "STEWARDESSES" IS THE LONGEST WORD YOU CAN TYPE USING ONLY YOUR LEFT HAND ON A STANDARD KEYBOARD.

1220 "RACECAR" IS A PALINDROME, MEANING IT IS SPELLED THE EXACT SAME FORWARDS AND BACKWARDS.

1221 THE WORD "UMBRELLA" COMES FROM THE LATIN WORD "UMBRA," WHICH MEANS SHADE.

1222 EVERY SINGLE ODD NUMBER HAS THE LETTER "E" IN IT.

1223 THE NUMBER "ONE" IS THE ONLY NUMBER WITH ITS LETTERS IN REVERSE ALPHABETICAL ORDER.

1224 THE WORD "ALPHABET" COMES FROM COMBINING THE FIRST TWO LETTERS OF THE GREEK ALPHABET: ALPHA AND BETA.

1225 THE WORD "SCHOOL" COMES FROM AN ANCIENT GREEK WORD MEANING "FREE TIME".

1226 THE FEAR OF THE NUMBER 13 IS CALLED TRISKAIDEKAPHOBIA.

1227 THE FEAR THAT A DUCK IS SOMEHOW WATCHING YOU IS CALLED ANATIDAEPHOBIA.

1228 CHEROPHOBIA IS THE IRRATIONAL FEAR OF BEING HAPPY.

1229 STARBUCKS IS NAMED AFTER STARBUCK, A CHARACTER IN THE CLASSIC BOOK MOBY DICK.

1230 THE FIRST HARRY POTTER BOOK WAS REJECTED BY 12 DIFFERENT PUBLISHERS BEFORE IT FINALLY GOT PRINTED.

1231 DR. SEUSS INVENTED THE WORD "NERD" IN HIS 1950 BOOK IF I RAN THE ZOO.

1232 IF YOU WRITE OUT EVERY NUMBER NAME IN ORDER (ONE, TWO, THREE...), YOU WON'T USE THE LETTER "B" UNTIL YOU REACH ONE BILLION.

1233 "GRIFFONAGE" IS A WORD USED TO DESCRIBE COMPLETELY ILLEGIBLE HANDWRITING.

1234 "PHOSPHENES" IS THE SCIENTIFIC NAME FOR THE COLORS AND STARS YOU SEE WHEN YOU RUB YOUR EYES.

1235 "DEFENESTRATION" IS A SPECIFIC WORD THAT MEANS "THE ACT OF THROWING SOMEONE OUT OF A WINDOW".

1236 THE WORD "ASTRONAUT" COMES FROM ANCIENT GREEK WORDS MEANING "STAR SAILOR".

1237 THE WORD "HIPPOPOTAMUS" TRANSLATES DIRECTLY TO "RIVER HORSE".

1238 THE WORD "RHINOCEROS" TRANSLATES DIRECTLY TO "NOSE HORN".

1239 THE WORD "DINOSAUR" TRANSLATES DIRECTLY TO "TERRIBLE LIZARD".

1240 THE WORD "PLANET" COMES FROM A GREEK WORD MEANING "WANDERER".

1241 THE WORD "ARCTIC" COMES FROM THE GREEK WORD FOR "BEAR," REFERRING TO THE CONSTELLATION URSA MAJOR.

1242 THE WORD "ANTARCTICA" SIMPLY MEANS "OPPOSITE THE BEAR".

1243 THE WORD "GOODBYE" IS A HEAVILY SHORTENED VERSION OF THE OLD PHRASE "GOD BE WITH YE".

1244 THE WORD "SWIMS" LOOKS EXACTLY THE SAME WHEN YOU TURN IT COMPLETELY UPSIDE DOWN.

1245 A "FORTNIGHT" IS A SPECIFIC HISTORICAL UNIT OF TIME EQUAL TO TWO WEEKS.

1246 THE LONGEST PLACE NAME IN THE UK IS A VILLAGE IN WALES CALLED LLANFAIRPWLLGWYNGYLLGOGERYCHWYRN-DROBWLLLLANTYSILIOGOGOGOCH.

1247 TAUMATAWHAKATANGIHANGAKOAUAUOTAMATEATURIPU-KAKAPIKIMAUNGAHORONUKUPOKAIWHENUAKITANATAHU IS A HILL IN NEW ZEALAND THAT HOLDS THE RECORD FOR THE LONGEST PLACE NAME IN THE WORLD.

1248 BANGKOK'S FULL OFFICIAL CEREMONIAL NAME IS 168 LETTERS LONG.

1249 THE JAPANESE WORD "KARAOKE" TRANSLATES DIRECTLY TO "EMPTY ORCHESTRA".

1250 IN THE POLISH VERSION OF THE BOARD GAME SCRABBLE, THE LETTER Z IS SURPRISINGLY ONLY WORTH ONE POINT.

1251 THE TRADITIONAL HAWAIIAN ALPHABET ONLY HAS 13 LETTERS.

1252 THE WORD "OXYMORON" IS ITSELF AN OXYMORON; IN ANCIENT GREEK, "OXY" MEANS SHARP AND "MORON" MEANS DULL.

1253 THERE IS A WORD FOR THE FEAR OF POETRY: METROPHOBIA.

1254 THE MOST COMMONLY USED NOUN IN THE ENGLISH LANGUAGE IS THE WORD 'TIME'.

1255 THE WORD 'LISTEN' CONTAINS THE EXACT SAME LETTERS AS THE WORD 'SILENT'.

1256 THE FIRST DICTIONARY OF THE ENGLISH LANGUAGE WAS PUBLISHED IN 1755 AND TOOK NINE YEARS TO WRITE.

1257 J.R.R. TOLKIEN INVENTED ENTIRE LANGUAGES, INCLUDING ELVISH, BEFORE HE EVEN WROTE THE STORIES OF MIDDLE-EARTH.

1258 THE MOST TRANSLATED BOOK IN THE WORLD, OTHER THAN RELIGIOUS TEXTS, IS "THE LITTLE PRINCE" BY ANTOINE DE SAINT-EXUPÉRY.

1259 THE SENTENCE "THE QUICK BROWN FOX JUMPS OVER THE LAZY DOG" USES EVERY SINGLE LETTER IN THE ENGLISH ALPHABET.

1260 WILLIAM SHAKESPEARE IS CREDITED WITH INVENTING OVER 1,700 WORDS, INCLUDING "EYEBALL" AND "BEDROOM".

1261 A PANGRAM IS A SENTENCE THAT CONTAINS EVERY LETTER OF THE ALPHABET.

1262 THE LONGEST NOVEL EVER WRITTEN CONTAINS OVER 2 MILLION WORDS.

1263 BRAILLE IS NOT A LANGUAGE; IT IS A CODE USED TO WRITE DIFFERENT LANGUAGES SO THEY CAN BE READ BY TOUCH.

1264 THE ENGLISH LANGUAGE GROWS BY ABOUT 4,000 NEW WORDS EVERY YEAR.

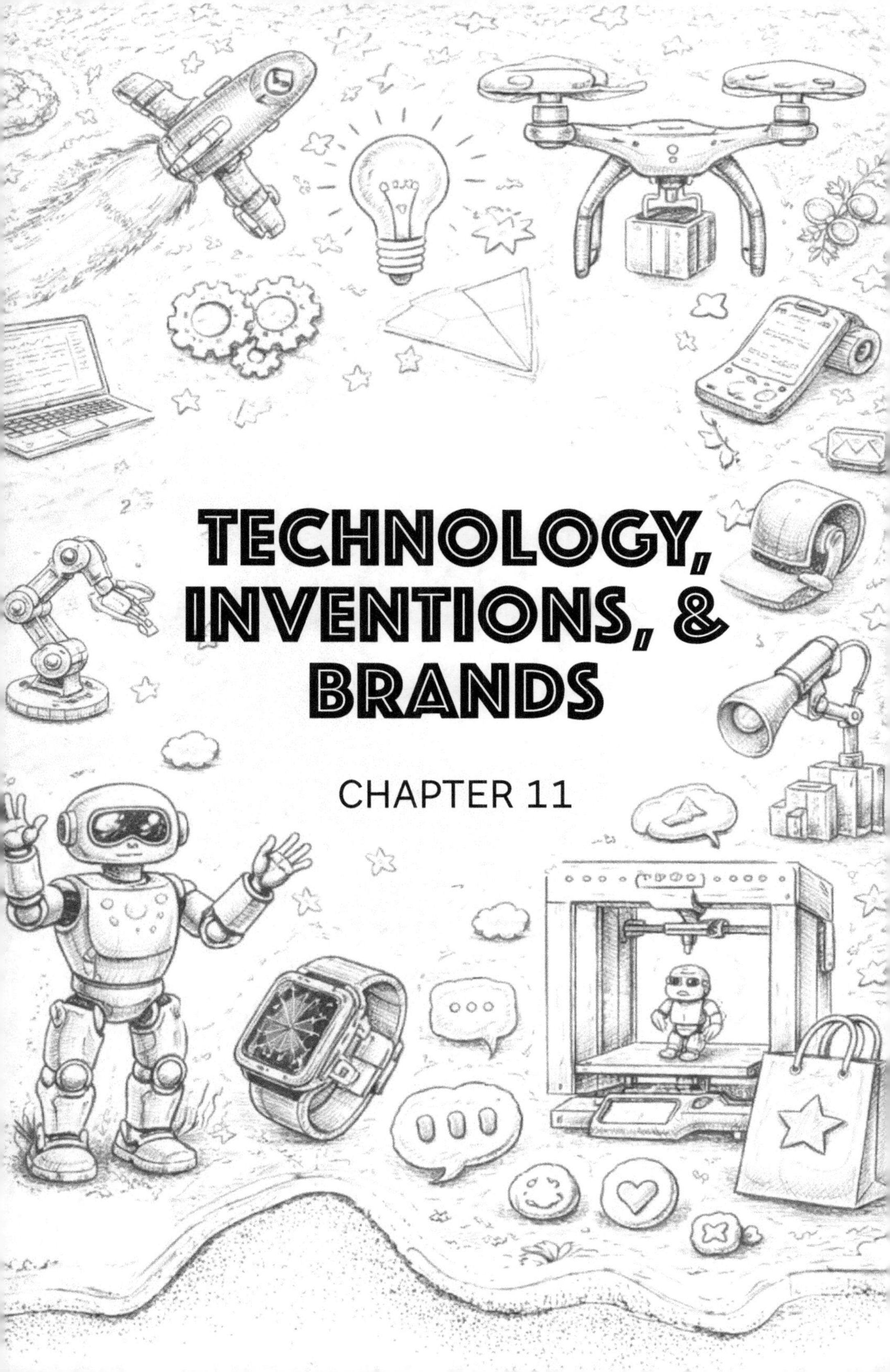

TECHNOLOGY, INVENTIONS, & BRANDS

CHAPTER 11

1265 IN 1903, THE WRIGHT BROTHERS FLEW FOR 59 SECONDS; JUST 66 YEARS LATER, HUMANS WALKED ON THE MOON.

1266 THE FIRST AIRPLANE FLIGHT LASTED ONLY 12 SECONDS.

1267 MORE THAN 85 PERCENT OF A TOYOTA PRIUS CAN BE RECYCLED.

1268 THE FIRST RECORDED ELECTRIC CAR WAS CREATED IN 1891.

1269 BUBBLE WRAP WAS ORIGINALLY INVENTED TO BE A TYPE OF 3D WALLPAPER.

1270 THE FIRST COMPUTER MOUSE WAS MADE OF WOOD.

1271 THE QWERTY KEYBOARD WAS ORIGINALLY DESIGNED TO SLOW TYPISTS DOWN SO THEIR TYPEWRITERS WOULDN'T JAM.

1272 BEFORE TOILET PAPER WAS INVENTED, AMERICANS USED CORN COBS.

1273 WINDSHIELD WIPERS WERE INVENTED BY A WOMAN NAMED MARY ANDERSON IN 1903.

1274 VOLVO INVENTED THE THREE-POINT SEATBELT, BUT THEY GAVE THE PATENT AWAY FOR FREE SO OTHER CAR COMPANIES COULD SAVE LIVES TOO.

1275 THE AVERAGE CAR SPENDS 95% OF ITS LIFE PARKED.

1276 WHITE IS THE MOST POPULAR CAR COLOR IN THE WORLD.

1277 THE AVERAGE CAR IS MADE UP OF ABOUT 30,000 UNIQUE PARTS.

1278 AIRBAGS DEPLOY AT SPEEDS OF UP TO 200 MILES PER HOUR.

1279 SILLY PUTTY WAS INVENTED BY ACCIDENT DURING WORLD WAR II WHEN SCIENTISTS WERE TRYING TO MAKE ARTIFICIAL RUBBER.

1280 HIGHLIGHTERS WERE ORIGINALLY MADE YELLOW BECAUSE THAT COLOR DOESN'T LEAVE A SHADOW WHEN PHOTOCOPIED.

1281 THE FIRST WEBCAM WAS INVENTED AT CAMBRIDGE UNIVERSITY JUST TO CHECK IF THE COFFEE POT WAS FULL WITHOUT GETTING UP.

1282 THE COLORS OF THE GOOGLE LOGO WERE CHOSEN TO SHOW THAT THE COMPANY DOESN'T FOLLOW THE RULES.

1283 AMAZON.COM WAS ORIGINALLY GOING TO BE NAMED "CADABRA", SHORT FOR ABRACADABRA.

1284 ZIPPERS WERE ORIGINALLY CALLED "CLASP LOCKERS".

1285 THE INVENTOR OF THE MICROWAVE RECEIVED ONLY $2 FOR HIS DISCOVERY.

1286 LIGHTERS WERE INVENTED BEFORE MATCHES.

1287 VENDING MACHINES KILL MORE PEOPLE EVERY YEAR THAN SHARKS DO.

1288 PLAY-DOH WAS ORIGINALLY INVENTED AS A WALLPAPER CLEANER.

1289 BLUETOOTH TECHNOLOGY IS NAMED AFTER A VIKING KING WHO UNITED THE TRIBES OF DENMARK AND NORWAY.

1290 THE FIRST COMPUTER "BUG" WAS A REAL MOTH TRAPPED IN A COMPUTER.

1291 EMAIL WAS INVENTED BEFORE THE WORLD WIDE WEB.

1292 YOUR SMARTPHONE HAS MORE COMPUTING POWER THAN THE COMPUTERS USED TO LAND APOLLO 11 ON THE MOON.

1293 MEMORY FOAM WAS ORIGINALLY INVENTED BY NASA TO PROTECT ASTRONAUTS DURING CRASHES.

1294 NASA INVENTED THE TECHNOLOGY USED IN SCRATCH-RESISTANT EYEGLASS LENSES.

1295 INVISIBLE BRACES WERE DEVELOPED FROM A MATERIAL NASA USED TO PROTECT RADAR EQUIPMENT.

1296 THE "SAVE" ICON IS A PICTURE OF A FLOPPY DISK, WHICH HASN'T BEEN USED IN DECADES.

1297 "SPAM" EMAIL IS NAMED AFTER A MONTY PYTHON SKETCH ABOUT PROCESSED MEAT.

1298 WD-40 STANDS FOR "WATER DISPLACEMENT, 40TH FORMULA".

1299 7-ELEVEN GOT ITS NAME BECAUSE THE STORES USED TO BE OPEN FROM 7 A.M. TO 11 P.M.

1300 THE FOUNDERS OF ADIDAS AND PUMA WERE BROTHERS WHO HAD A HUGE RIVALRY.

1301 LAMBORGHINI ORIGINALLY MADE TRACTORS BEFORE MAKING SPORTS CARS.

1302 POST-IT NOTES WERE INVENTED WHEN A SCIENTIST ACCIDENTALLY MADE GLUE THAT WASN'T STICKY ENOUGH.

1303 PENICILLIN WAS DISCOVERED BY ACCIDENT WHEN MOLD GREW IN A PETRI DISH.

1304 VELCRO WAS INVENTED AFTER A MAN NOTICED BURRS STICKING TO HIS DOG'S FUR.

1305 THE CHUPA CHUPS LOLLIPOP LOGO WAS DESIGNED BY THE FAMOUS ARTIST SALVADOR DALÍ.

1306 TREADMILLS WERE ORIGINALLY INVENTED TO PUNISH PRISONERS IN THE 1800S.

1307 BEFORE ALARM CLOCKS WERE COMMON, PEOPLE USED TO INSERT NAILS INTO CANDLES SO THEY WOULD CLATTER ONTO A METAL TRAY WHEN THE WAX MELTED DOWN.

1308 THE FIRST EMAIL EVER SENT WAS BY RAY TOMLINSON TO HIMSELF.

1309 THE COMPUTER MOUSE WAS NAMED BECAUSE THE CORD COMING OUT OF THE BACK LOOKED LIKE A TAIL.

1310 PENCILS ARE PAINTED YELLOW BECAUSE IN THE 1800S, THE BEST GRAPHITE CAME FROM CHINA, WHERE YELLOW IS A ROYAL COLOR.

1311 SUNGLASSES WERE ORIGINALLY WORN BY JUDGES IN ANCIENT CHINA TO HIDE THEIR FACIAL EXPRESSIONS IN COURT.

1312 THE BRISTLES OF THE FIRST TOOTHBRUSHES WERE MADE FROM STIFF HAIRS TAKEN FROM THE BACK OF A HOG'S NECK.

1313 VACUUM CLEANERS WERE ORIGINALLY INVENTED TO SUCK DUST OUT OF CARPETS, BUT THE FIRST ONES BLEW AIR INSTEAD OF SUCKING.

1314 X-RAYS WERE DISCOVERED BY ACCIDENT WHEN WILHELM RÖNTGEN NOTICED A GLOWING SCREEN IN HIS LAB.

1315 WI-FI DOESN'T ACTUALLY STAND FOR "WIRELESS FIDELITY"; THE CREATORS JUST THOUGHT IT SOUNDED CATCHY.

1316 THE FIRST NIKE SHOES WERE MADE INSIDE A WAFFLE IRON.

1317 SONY'S FIRST PRODUCT WAS AN ELECTRIC RICE COOKER THAT DIDN'T WORK VERY WELL.

1318 BEFORE MAKING PHONES, NOKIA MADE RUBBER BOOTS AND CAR TIRES.

1319 THE NAME "LEGO" COMES FROM THE DANISH PHRASE "LEG GODT," WHICH MEANS "PLAY WELL".

1320 THE "@" SYMBOL IS CALLED A "SNAIL" IN ITALY AND A "MONKEY TAIL" IN THE NETHERLANDS.

1321 THE COMPUTER CODE FOR THE APOLLO 11 MOON LANDING WAS WRITTEN BY HAND ON PAPER BEFORE BEING TYPED INTO THE COMPUTER.

1322 THE VERY FIRST TEXT MESSAGE EVER SENT SAID, "MERRY CHRISTMAS".

1323 EMOJIS WERE INVENTED IN JAPAN IN THE LATE 1990S.

1324 THE "TEARS OF JOY" EMOJI IS THE MOST USED EMOJI IN THE WORLD.

1325 YOUTUBE WAS ORIGINALLY DESIGNED TO BE A VIDEO DATING SITE BEFORE IT BECAME A PLACE FOR ALL VIDEOS.

1326 FACEBOOK IS BLUE BECAUSE ITS FOUNDER, MARK ZUCKERBERG, IS RED-GREEN COLORBLIND AND BLUE IS THE COLOR HE SEES BEST.

1327 INSTAGRAM WAS ORIGINALLY CALLED "BURBN".

1328 THE ENTIRE INTERNET WEIGHS ABOUT THE SAME AS A STRAWBERRY (IF YOU WEIGHED THE ELECTRONS THAT MAKE IT WORK).

1329 THERE ARE MORE MOBILE PHONES IN THE WORLD TODAY THAN THERE ARE TOOTHBRUSHES.

1330 THE "COMMAND" KEY SYMBOL ON APPLE KEYBOARDS IS ACTUALLY A SWEDISH ROAD SIGN FOR A CAMPGROUND.

1331 THE FAX MACHINE WAS INVENTED IN 1843, OVER 30 YEARS BEFORE THE TELEPHONE.

1332 THE BICYCLE WAS INVENTED AFTER THE STEAM TRAIN.

1333 HUMANS WENT TO THE MOON BEFORE WE THOUGHT TO PUT WHEELS ON SUITCASES.

1334 THE POM-POM ON TOP OF A BEANIE HAT WAS ORIGINALLY DESIGNED TO PROTECT SAILORS FROM HITTING THEIR HEADS IN TIGHT SPACES.

1335 THE BUTTONS ON THE SLEEVES OF MEN'S SUIT JACKETS WERE ORIGINALLY ADDED TO STOP SOLDIERS FROM WIPING THEIR NOSES ON THEIR SLEEVES.

1336 T-SHIRTS WERE ORIGINALLY INVENTED TO BE UNDERWEAR.

1337 BLUE JEANS WERE ORIGINALLY INVENTED FOR GOLD MINERS WHO NEEDED DURABLE PANTS.

1338 LISTERINE WAS ORIGINALLY SOLD AS A FLOOR CLEANER BEFORE IT BECAME MOUTHWASH.

1339 NIKE IS NAMED AFTER THE GREEK GODDESS OF VICTORY.

1340 THE CAMERA COMPANY CANON WAS ORIGINALLY NAMED "KWANON" AFTER A BUDDHIST FIGURE.

1341 SAMSUNG MEANS "THREE STARS" IN KOREAN.

1342 VOLKSWAGEN TRANSLATES TO "PEOPLE'S CAR" IN GERMAN.

1343 THE CAR BRAND AUDI IS THE LATIN TRANSLATION OF THE FOUNDER'S LAST NAME, "HORCH," WHICH MEANS "LISTEN".

1344 BMW STANDS FOR BAVARIAN MOTOR WORKS.

1345 PRINGLES ARE NOT TECHNICALLY "POTATO CHIPS" BECAUSE THEY ARE MADE FROM DEHYDRATED POTATO DOUGH, NOT SLICED POTATOES.

1346 THE MASCOT ON THE PRINGLES CAN HAS A NAME: JULIUS PRINGLES.

1347 THE LOGO FOR THE WEB BROWSER FIREFOX IS ACTUALLY A RED PANDA, NOT A FOX.

1348 THE DESIGNER OF THE NIKE "SWOOSH" LOGO WAS A STUDENT WHO WAS PAID ONLY $35 FOR IT.

1349 THE FIRST ELECTRONIC COMPUTER, ENIAC, WEIGHED 27 TONS AND TOOK UP AN ENTIRE ROOM.

1350 99% OF THE WORLD'S INTERNET DATA TRAVELS THROUGH CABLES RUNNING UNDERWATER AT THE BOTTOM OF THE OCEAN.

1351 ALEXANDER GRAHAM BELL WANTED PEOPLE TO ANSWER THE TELEPHONE BY SAYING "AHOY".

1352 KLEENEX TISSUES WERE ORIGINALLY INVENTED TO BE USED AS GAS MASK FILTERS DURING WORLD WAR I.

1353 IN COMPUTER LANGUAGE, A "BYTE" IS MADE OF 8 BITS, BUT HALF A BYTE IS OFFICIALLY CALLED A "NIBBLE".

1354 THE SCREECHING SOUND OF AN OLD DIAL-UP MODEM WAS ACTUALLY TWO COMPUTERS SENDING DATA TO EACH OTHER.

1355 THE FIRST ITEM EVER SOLD ON EBAY WAS A BROKEN LASER POINTER.

1356 AMAZON BEGAN AS AN ONLINE BOOKSTORE.

1357 GOOGLE WAS ORIGINALLY CALLED "BACKRUB".

1358 NINTENDO WAS FOUNDED IN 1889 AS A PLAYING CARD COMPANY.

1359 THE FIRST 3D MOVIE WAS SHOWN TO AN AUDIENCE IN A THEATER ALL THE WAY BACK IN 1922.

1360 THE FIRST PERSON TO WALK ON THE MOON, NEIL ARMSTRONG, CARRIED A PIECE OF WOOD FROM THE WRIGHT BROTHERS' FIRST AIRPLANE IN HIS SPACE SUIT POCKET.

1361 THE VERY FIRST APPLE COMPUTER, THE APPLE I, WAS BUILT BY HAND OUT OF WOOD.

1362 THE VERY FIRST ALARM CLOCK COULD ONLY RING AT 4:00 AM.

1363 THE FIRST DOMAIN NAME EVER REGISTERED ON THE INTERNET WAS SYMBOLICS.COM IN 1985.

1364 THE AVERAGE COMPUTER USER BLINKS 7 TIMES A MINUTE, WHICH IS LESS THAN HALF THE NORMAL RATE.

1365 THE ORIGINAL XBOX CONSOLE WAS GOING TO BE CALLED THE "DIRECTX BOX".

1366 GPS TECHNOLOGY IS FREE FOR EVERYONE TO USE, BUT IT COSTS THE U.S. GOVERNMENT ABOUT $2 MILLION A DAY TO OPERATE.

1367 THE QR CODE WAS ORIGINALLY INVENTED IN JAPAN TO TRACK VEHICLES DURING THE MANUFACTURING PROCESS.

1368 THE FIRST VIDEO GAME EVER CREATED WAS A SIMPLE TENNIS GAME CALLED TENNIS FOR TWO IN 1958.

1369 THE FIRST DIGITAL CAMERA WAS INVENTED IN 1975, WEIGHED 8 POUNDS, AND TOOK 23 SECONDS TO RECORD A SINGLE BLACK-AND-WHITE IMAGE.

1370 THE CLASSIC "NOKIA TUNE" RINGTONE IS ACTUALLY BASED ON A GUITAR PIECE WRITTEN IN THE 19TH CENTURY.

1371 THE FIRST ITEM EVER SCANNED WITH A BARCODE WAS A PACK OF WRIGLEY'S JUICY FRUIT CHEWING GUM IN 1974.

1372 THERE IS 100 TIMES MORE GOLD IN A TON OF SMARTPHONES THAN IN A TON OF RAW GOLD ORE.

1373 CAPTCHA IS ACTUALLY AN ACRONYM THAT STANDS FOR "COMPLETELY AUTOMATED PUBLIC TURING TEST TO TELL COMPUTERS AND HUMANS APART".

1374 THE VERY FIRST VIDEO EVER UPLOADED TO YOUTUBE IS AN 18-SECOND CLIP OF A CO-FOUNDER STANDING IN FRONT OF ELEPHANTS CALLED "ME AT THE ZOO".

1375 STEVE JOBS WAS BRIEFLY ASSIGNED TO THE NIGHT SHIFT AT ATARI BECAUSE HIS COWORKERS CONSTANTLY COMPLAINED ABOUT HIS POOR HYGIENE.

1376 THE FIRST MOBILE PHONE CALL WAS MADE IN 1973 BY A MOTOROLA ENGINEER SPECIFICALLY TO BRAG TO HIS DIRECT RIVAL AT BELL LABS.

1377 TWITTER'S ORIGINAL BLUE BIRD LOGO WAS OFFICIALLY NAMED "LARRY THE BIRD" IN HONOR OF THE FAMOUS BASKETBALL PLAYER.

1378 PEPSI WAS ORIGINALLY SOLD IN 1893 UNDER THE NAME "BRAD'S DRINK" BY ITS CREATOR, CALEB BRADHAM.

1379 THERE IS A HIDDEN, FULLY FUNCTIONAL FLIGHT SIMULATOR BUILT DIRECTLY INTO THE GOOGLE EARTH PROGRAM.

1380 MATCHBOX CARS GOT THEIR NAME BECAUSE THE CREATOR'S DAUGHTER WAS ONLY ALLOWED TO BRING TOYS TO SCHOOL IF THEY PHYSICALLY FIT INSIDE A REAL MATCHBOX.

1381 THE CLASSIC COMPUTER GAME "MINESWEEPER" WAS INCLUDED IN EARLY WINDOWS SOFTWARE PRIMARILY TO TEACH USERS HOW TO COMFORTABLY LEFT- AND RIGHT-CLICK A MOUSE.

1382 TEFLON, THE FAMOUS NON-STICK COATING ON PANS, WAS DISCOVERED COMPLETELY BY ACCIDENT BY SCIENTISTS TRYING TO INVENT A NEW REFRIGERATOR COOLANT.

1383 THE VERY FIRST APPLE COMPUTER LOGO DID NOT LOOK LIKE AN APPLE; IT WAS A HIGHLY DETAILED INK DRAWING OF ISAAC NEWTON SITTING UNDER AN APPLE TREE.

1384 THE ICONIC MACINTOSH STARTUP CHIME WAS SPECIFICALLY DESIGNED TO STRIKE A SOOTHING CHORD TO REASSURE USERS THAT THE COMPUTER HADN'T CRASHED WHILE TURNING ON.

1385 THE FIRST COMPUTER HARD DRIVE WAS CREATED BY IBM IN 1956, HELD ONLY 5 MEGABYTES OF DATA, AND WAS THE SIZE OF TWO LARGE REFRIGERATORS.

1386 BEFORE IT WAS KNOWN AS THE MASSIVELY POPULAR MESSAGING APP, SNAPCHAT WAS ORIGINALLY LAUNCHED UNDER THE NAME "PICABOO".

1387 THE FIRST MECHANICAL SLOT MACHINE, THE LIBERTY BELL, WAS INVENTED BY A CAR MECHANIC IN 1895 TO KEEP HIS CUSTOMERS ENTERTAINED WHILE WAITING FOR REPAIRS.

1388 THE CREATOR OF THE USB FLASH DRIVE INVENTED THE DEVICE OUT OF PURE FRUSTRATION AFTER HIS LAPTOP DIED RIGHT BEFORE A MAJOR PRESENTATION.

POP, MUSIC & CULTURE

CHAPTER 12

1389 THE OSCARS RED CARPET ISN'T ACTUALLY RED; IT IS A CUSTOM SHADE CALLED "ACADEMY RED" DESIGNED TO LOOK BEST ON TELEVISION CAMERAS.

1390 THE SOUND OF THE VELOCIRAPTORS COMMUNICATING WITH EACH OTHER IN THE MOVIE JURASSIC PARK WAS MADE BY RECORDING TORTOISES MATING.

1391 THE FAMOUS FALLING GREEN CODE IN THE MOVIE THE MATRIX IS ACTUALLY JUST A SCANNED SUSHI RECIPE FROM A JAPANESE COOKBOOK.

1392 WALT DISNEY REFUSED TO LET DIRECTOR ALFRED HITCHCOCK FILM AT DISNEYLAND BECAUSE HE HAD RECENTLY MADE "THAT DISGUSTING MOVIE PSYCHO".

1393 THE VOICE ACTOR FOR MICKEY MOUSE AND THE VOICE ACTOR FOR MINNIE MOUSE ACTUALLY GOT MARRIED IN REAL LIFE.

1394 THE DISNEY MOVIE THE LION KING WAS ORIGINALLY GOING TO BE CALLED KING OF THE JUNGLE, UNTIL THE CREATORS REALIZED LIONS DON'T ACTUALLY LIVE IN THE JUNGLE.

1395 IN THE MOVIE E.T. THE EXTRA-TERRESTRIAL, THE SQUISHY SOUND OF E.T. WALKING WAS MADE BY SOMEONE SHOVING THEIR HANDS INTO A LARGE BOWL OF JELL-O.

1396 THE TERRIFYING MASK WORN BY MICHAEL MYERS IN THE MOVIE HALLOWEEN IS ACTUALLY A CHEAP CAPTAIN KIRK (WILLIAM SHATNER) MASK SPRAY-PAINTED WHITE.

1397 YODA'S FACE IN STAR WARS WAS PARTIALLY MODELED AFTER THE FAMOUS SCIENTIST ALBERT EINSTEIN TO MAKE HIM LOOK INTELLIGENT.

1398 STAN LEE ALMOST NAMED SPIDER-MAN "FLY-MAN," AND ENVISIONED HIM SHOOTING WEBS OUT OF A MAGIC RING RATHER THAN HIS WRISTS.

1399 THE "WILHELM SCREAM" IS A FAMOUS STOCK SOUND EFFECT OF A MAN YELLING THAT HAS BEEN SECRETLY USED IN OVER 400 MOVIES, INCLUDING STAR WARS AND INDIANA JONES.

1400 IN THE ORIGINAL SCRIPT FOR TOY STORY, WOODY WAS WRITTEN TO BE A CRUEL, SARCASTIC, AND BOSSY VENTRILOQUIST DUMMY.

1401 IN THE CARTOON SPONGEBOB SQUAREPANTS, THE KRUSTY KRAB RESTAURANT IS PHYSICALLY SHAPED LIKE A REAL-LIFE LOBSTER TRAP.

1402 THE ICONIC "DUN-DUN" SOUND EFFECT IN THE TV SHOW LAW & ORDER WAS CREATED BY COMBINING THE SOUNDS OF A JUDGE'S GAVEL AND A HEAVY JAIL CELL DOOR SLAMMING SHUT.

1403 THE PIXAR MOVIE UP FEATURES EXACTLY 20,622 INDIVIDUAL ANIMATED BALLOONS TIED TO CARL'S HOUSE WHEN IT TAKES OFF.

1404 THE CREATOR OF THE COMIC STRIP GARFIELD NAMED THE LAZY, LASAGNA-LOVING CAT AFTER HIS OWN GRANDFATHER, JAMES GARFIELD DAVIS.

1405 THE TERRIFYING SOUND OF THE T-REX'S ROAR IN JURASSIC PARK IS A LAYERED COMBINATION OF A BABY ELEPHANT, A TIGER, AND AN ALLIGATOR.

1406 THE LONGEST-RUNNING ANIMATED TELEVISION SHOW IN HISTORY IS THE SIMPSONS, WHICH PREMIERED ALL THE WAY BACK IN 1989.

1407 HARRY POTTER ACTOR DANIEL RADCLIFFE WENT THROUGH 160 DIFFERENT PAIRS OF PROP GLASSES WHILE FILMING THE EIGHT MOVIES.

1408 THE NAME "SHREK" COMES FROM THE YIDDISH WORD MEANING "MONSTER" OR "TERROR".

1409 AT JUST 16 YEARS OLD, SOCCER STAR LAMINE YAMAL BECAME SUCH A MASSIVE GLOBAL POP CULTURE PHENOMENON THAT HIS SIGNATURE GOAL CELEBRATION INSTANTLY WENT VIRAL ACROSS TIKTOK.

1410 THE FAMOUS PIZZA PLANET TRUCK FROM TOY STORY IS HIDDEN AS AN EASTER EGG IN ALMOST EVERY SINGLE PIXAR MOVIE.

1411 SULLEY FROM MONSTERS, INC. HAS OVER 2.3 MILLION INDIVIDUALLY ANIMATED HAIRS, WHICH TOOK SUPERCOMPUTERS HOURS TO PROCESS FOR A SINGLE FRAME.

1412 GODZILLA'S ICONIC ROAR WAS ORIGINALLY MADE BY RUBBING A LEATHER GLOVE COATED IN PINE TAR AGAINST A DOUBLE BASS STRING.

1413 TOM CRUISE HELD HIS BREATH UNDERWATER FOR A STAGGERING SIX MINUTES FOR A STUNT IN THE MOVIE MISSION: IMPOSSIBLE - ROGUE NATION.

1414 THE 1997 MOVIE TITANIC ACTUALLY COST MORE MONEY TO MAKE THAN THE REAL-LIFE TITANIC SHIP COST TO BUILD.

1415 ACTION STAR JACKIE CHAN BROKE SO MANY BONES DOING HIS OWN DANGEROUS MOVIE STUNTS THAT HE IS OFFICIALLY UNINSURABLE FOR FILM PRODUCTIONS IN THE UNITED STATES.

1416 IN THE WIZARD OF OZ, THE FAKE SNOW THAT FALLS ON DOROTHY IN THE POPPY FIELD WAS DANGEROUSLY MADE OF 100% PURE ASBESTOS.

1417 THE VERY FIRST TOILET EVER SHOWN FLUSHING ON AMERICAN TELEVISION WAS IN AN EPISODE OF THE SHOW LEAVE IT TO BEAVER.

1418 THE CREATORS OF STRANGER THINGS ORIGINALLY PLANNED TO KILL OFF THE POPULAR CHARACTER STEVE HARRINGTON IN SEASON ONE.

1419 THE SOUND OF THE IRON MAN SUIT'S BLASTERS FIRING WAS MADE BY HITTING A METAL SLINKY AND RECORDING THE ECHO.

1420 THE FICTIONAL WAKANDAN LANGUAGE SPOKEN IN BLACK PANTHER IS ACTUALLY A REAL, FUNCTIONING LANGUAGE CALLED XHOSA.

1421 GROOT FROM GUARDIANS OF THE GALAXY WAS PERSONALLY VOICED BY ACTOR VIN DIESEL IN 15 DIFFERENT LANGUAGES.

1422 THE EWOK LANGUAGE IN STAR WARS IS A BLENDED MIX OF TIBETAN AND NEPALI.

1423 IN ALADDIN, JASMINE'S FACIAL FEATURES AND APPEARANCE WERE HEAVILY INFLUENCED BY ACTRESS JENNIFER CONNELLY.

1424 WILL SMITH FAMOUSLY TURNED DOWN THE LEAD ROLE OF NEO IN THE MATRIX SO HE COULD STAR IN THE BOX-OFFICE FLOP WILD WILD WEST.

1425 A SINGLE FRAME OF THE STOP-MOTION MOVIE CORALINE TOOK ANIMATORS UP TO TWO HOURS TO CAREFULLY SET UP AND SHOOT.

1426 THE MINIONS LANGUAGE IS A BIZARRE MIX OF FRENCH, SPANISH, ENGLISH, AND RANDOM FOOD WORDS LIKE "POULET TIKI MASALA".

1427 IN SPIDER-MAN: INTO THE SPIDER-VERSE, IT TOOK A MASSIVE TEAM OF 177 ANIMATORS TO CREATE THE FILM'S UNIQUE COMIC-BOOK STYLE.

1428 AVATAR WAS ORIGINALLY SUPPOSED TO BE FILMED IN 1999, BUT DIRECTOR JAMES CAMERON HAD TO WAIT A DECADE BECAUSE THE REQUIRED CGI TECHNOLOGY DIDN'T EXIST YET.

1429 THE VERY FIRST MUSIC VIDEO EVER BROADCAST ON MTV WAS APPROPRIATELY TITLED "VIDEO KILLED THE RADIO STAR" BY THE BUGGLES.

1430 RAPPER EMINEM'S HIT SONG "RAP GOD" HOLDS A WORLD RECORD FOR PACKING 1,560 WORDS INTO JUST OVER SIX MINUTES.

1431 THE LONGEST PIECE OF MUSIC EVER WRITTEN IS DESIGNED TO PLAY CONTINUOUSLY FOR 1,000 YEARS; IT STARTED PLAYING IN 1999 AND WILL FINISH IN THE YEAR 2999.

1432 THE COMPOSER BEETHOVEN USED TO DIP HIS HEAD INTO A BUCKET OF FREEZING COLD WATER BEFORE HE WROTE MUSIC TO STIMULATE HIS BRAIN.

1433 POP STAR ARIANA GRANDE'S SIGNATURE LONG PONYTAIL WAS ORIGINALLY A HAIRPIECE SHE WORE BECAUSE HER REAL HAIR WAS SEVERELY DAMAGED FROM DYING IT RED FOR A TV SHOW.

1434 THE ORIGINAL NAME FOR THE POP-ROCK BAND MAROON 5 WAS "KARA'S FLOWERS".

1435 TAYLOR SWIFT WROTE HER OWN 350-PAGE FICTION NOVEL WHEN SHE WAS JUST 12 YEARS OLD, THOUGH SHE HAS NEVER PUBLISHED IT.

1436 RAPPER SNOOP DOGG HAS AN ABNORMALLY HIGH IQ OF 147, MAKING HIM A CERTIFIED GENIUS.

1437 THE HIGHEST MUSICAL NOTE EVER SUNG BY A HUMAN IS A G10, WHICH IS SO INCREDIBLY HIGH IT SOUNDS EXACTLY LIKE A DOG WHISTLE.

1438 THE CHILDREN'S SONG "BABY SHARK" IS THE MOST-WATCHED VIDEO IN THE HISTORY OF YOUTUBE, WITH OVER 14 BILLION VIEWS.

1439 BILLIE EILISH RECORDED HER ENTIRE GRAMMY-WINNING DEBUT ALBUM NOT IN A FANCY STUDIO, BUT SITTING ON A BED IN HER BROTHER'S SMALL CHILDHOOD BEDROOM.

1440 IN 2012, A HIGHLY REALISTIC HOLOGRAM OF THE LATE RAPPER TUPAC SHAKUR SHOCKED AUDIENCES WHEN IT "PERFORMED" LIVE ON STAGE AT THE COACHELLA MUSIC FESTIVAL.

1441 THE BEATLES HOLD THE ALL-TIME RECORD FOR THE MOST NUMBER-ONE HITS ON THE BILLBOARD HOT 100 CHART.

1442 K-POP GROUP BTS WAS THE VERY FIRST KOREAN ACT TO TOP THE US BILLBOARD 200 CHART.

1443 THE WORLD'S LARGEST DRUM KIT HAS OVER 800 PIECES AND TAKES FOUR PEOPLE OVER AN HOUR JUST TO SET UP.

1444 STUDIES HAVE SHOWN THAT SOME PLANTS WILL ACTUALLY GROW FASTER AND HEALTHIER IF THEY LISTEN TO MUSIC.

1445 THE FAMOUS "CHILL LOFI BEATS TO STUDY TO" ANIME GIRL ON YOUTUBE HAS AN OFFICIAL NAME: SHIZUKU.

1446 METALLICA IS THE ONLY BAND IN HISTORY TO HAVE PLAYED A LIVE CONCERT ON ALL SEVEN CONTINENTS, INCLUDING ANTARCTICA.

1447 FREDDIE MERCURY OF QUEEN USED A PIANO AS A HEADBOARD FOR HIS BED AND LEARNED TO PLAY IT BACKWARDS SO HE COULD WRITE SONGS WHILE LYING DOWN.

1448 THE ICONIC "AMEN BREAK," A 6-SECOND DRUM SOLO RECORDED IN 1969, IS THE MOST LEGALLY AND ILLEGALLY SAMPLED TRACK IN MUSIC HISTORY.

1449 LIL NAS X BOUGHT THE BEAT FOR HIS RECORD-BREAKING HIT "OLD TOWN ROAD" FROM AN ONLINE BEAT STORE FOR JUST $30.

1450 POST MALONE'S FIRST MAJOR FORAY INTO LEARNING MUSIC WAS PLAYING THE VIDEO GAME GUITAR HERO ON EXPERT MODE.

1451 STRADIVARIUS VIOLINS ARE WORTH MILLIONS BECAUSE MODERN SCIENTISTS STILL CANNOT FIGURE OUT EXACTLY HOW THE WOOD WAS TREATED IN THE 1700S TO MAKE THEM SOUND SO GOOD.

1452 LEO FENDER, THE INVENTOR OF THE WORLD-FAMOUS FENDER STRATOCASTER ELECTRIC GUITAR, DIDN'T ACTUALLY KNOW HOW TO PLAY THE GUITAR.

1453 "WEIRD AL" YANKOVIC IS LEGALLY ALLOWED TO PARODY SONGS WITHOUT PERMISSION, BUT HE ALWAYS ASKS THE ORIGINAL ARTISTS FIRST OUT OF RESPECT.

1454 THE KAZOO WAS INVENTED IN THE 1840S IN THE STATE OF GEORGIA, USA.

1455 A PIANO COVERS THE FULL RANGE OF INSTRUMENTS IN AN ORCHESTRA, WHICH IS WHY IT REQUIRES EXACTLY 88 KEYS.

1456 ELVIS PRESLEY, THE KING OF ROCK AND ROLL, ONLY EVER WON THREE GRAMMY AWARDS IN HIS LIFE, AND THEY WERE ALL FOR GOSPEL MUSIC.

1457 DURING THE PANDEMIC IN 2021, 19TH-CENTURY SEA SHANTIES BECAME A MASSIVE, VIRAL MUSIC TREND ON TIKTOK.

1458 THE MUSICAL INSTRUMENT KNOWN AS A "THEREMIN" IS INCREDIBLY UNIQUE BECAUSE IT IS PLAYED WITHOUT THE MUSICIAN EVER ACTUALLY TOUCHING IT.

1459 THE FAMOUS TV PAINTER BOB ROSS KEPT A BABY ALLIGATOR IN AN EMPTY BATHTUB AS A PET WHEN HE WAS A KID.

1460 THE SMELL OF CRAYOLA CRAYONS IS OFFICIALLY RECOGNIZED AS ONE OF THE 20 MOST RECOGNIZABLE SCENTS TO AMERICAN ADULTS.

1461 THE COLOR "MUMMY BROWN" WAS AN ACTUAL PAINT COLOR USED BY ARTISTS IN THE 16TH TO 19TH CENTURIES, MADE FROM REAL, GROUND-UP EGYPTIAN MUMMIES.

1462 LEONARDO DA VINCI USED TO BUY CAGED BIRDS AND ANIMALS AT THE LOCAL MARKET JUST SO HE COULD OPEN THE DOORS AND SET THEM FREE.

1463 THE MOST EXPENSIVE PAINTING EVER SOLD IN HISTORY IS A PORTRAIT BY LEONARDO DA VINCI CALLED SALVATOR MUNDI, WHICH SOLD FOR $450 MILLION.

1464 THE FAMOUS PAINTING AMERICAN GOTHIC (THE STOIC FARMER AND WOMAN HOLDING A PITCHFORK) ACTUALLY FEATURES THE ARTIST'S SISTER AND HIS LOCAL DENTIST POSING AS THE MODELS.

1465 THE VERY FIRST FICTIONAL CHARACTER TO EVER BE AWARDED A STAR ON THE HOLLYWOOD WALK OF FAME WAS MICKEY MOUSE IN 1978.

1466 THE FAMOUS "WALK OF FAME" STARS IN HOLLYWOOD ARE NOT AWARDS; THEY COST AROUND $50,000 TO INSTALL AND MAINTAIN, AND THE CELEBRITIES HAVE TO PAY THE BILL THEMSELVES.

1467 THE ANONYMOUS STREET ARTIST BANKSY ONCE BUILT A HIDDEN PAPER SHREDDER INTO A PICTURE FRAME SO HIS PAINTING WOULD DESTROY ITSELF THE EXACT MOMENT IT WAS SOLD AT AUCTION.

1468 STREET ART WAS WIDELY CONSIDERED ILLEGAL GRAFFITI FOR DECADES UNTIL MODERN MURALISM TURNED IT INTO CELEBRATED CITY LANDMARKS.

1469 THE VERY FIRST MEME ON THE INTERNET IS WIDELY CONSIDERED TO BE THE VIRAL 3D DANCING BABY ANIMATION FROM 1996.

1470 THE FAMOUS "DOGE" INTERNET MEME FEATURES A REAL RESCUE SHIBA INU NAMED KABOSU FROM JAPAN.

1471 A PIECE OF MODERN ART CONSISTING OF A SINGLE, REAL BANANA DUCT-TAPED TO A WHITE WALL SOLD FOR $120,000 AT AN ART SHOW.

1472 THE VIRAL "RICKROLL" PRANK—TRICKING PEOPLE INTO CLICKING A LINK TO RICK ASTLEY'S "NEVER GONNA GIVE YOU UP"—STARTED IN 2007 ON AN ONLINE GAMING FORUM.

1473 THE ORIGINAL "NYAN CAT" ANIMATION WAS SOLD AS CERTIFIED DIGITAL ART FOR NEARLY $600,000.

1474 THE FAMOUS "DISASTER GIRL" MEME (A GIRL SMILING DEVIOUSLY WHILE A HOUSE BURNS IN THE BACKGROUND) WAS JUST A PHOTO TAKEN BY HER DAD AT A LOCAL FIRE DEPARTMENT TRAINING EXERCISE.

1475 THE INTERNET PHENOMENON OF "BRAINROT" REFERS TO HYPER-FAST, CHAOTIC MEME TRENDS THAT CYCLE SO QUICKLY THEY SEEM TO MAKE NO SENSE TO ANYONE NOT IN ON THE JOKE.

1476 THE PAINTER SALVADOR DALÍ ONCE GAVE A GUEST LECTURE WEARING A HEAVY DEEP-SEA DIVING SUIT, BUT HE ALMOST SUFFOCATED BECAUSE HE FORGOT TO HOOK UP THE OXYGEN.

1477 CLAUDE MONET PAINTED HIS MOST FAMOUS WATER LILIES WHILE HIS EYESIGHT WAS SEVERELY FADING FROM CATARACTS.

1478 PABLO PICASSO'S FULL BIRTH NAME IS INCREDIBLY LONG, CLOCKING IN AT 23 DIFFERENT WORDS.

1479 IN 2014, A JANITOR IN AN ART GALLERY IN ITALY ACCIDENTALLY THREW AWAY A MODERN ART EXHIBIT BECAUSE HE THOUGHT IT WAS JUST LEFTOVER TRASH FROM A PARTY THE NIGHT BEFORE.

1480 THE ICONIC "HOPE" POSTER OF BARACK OBAMA WAS CREATED BY A FAMOUS STREET ARTIST NAMED SHEPARD FAIREY.

1481 IT TOOK MICHELANGELO FOUR GRUELING YEARS TO PAINT THE CEILING OF THE SISTINE CHAPEL, AND HE HAD TO DO IT STANDING UP, NOT LYING ON HIS BACK.

1482 THE VIRAL "CHARLIE BIT MY FINGER" VIDEO WAS ORIGINALLY ONLY UPLOADED TO YOUTUBE BECAUSE THE VIDEO FILE WAS TOO BIG TO EMAIL TO THE BOYS' GODFATHER.

1483 ANDY WARHOL'S FAMOUS SOUP CAN PAINTINGS WERE PROJECTED ONTO THE CANVAS AND MANUALLY TRACED TO MAKE THEM LOOK PERFECTLY UNIFORM.

1484 THE COLOR "VANTABLACK" IS A MODERN ART MATERIAL SO DARK IT ABSORBS 99.96% OF LIGHT, MAKING 3D OBJECTS LOOK COMPLETELY FLAT LIKE A BLACK HOLE.

1485 THE ORIGINAL "TROLLFACE" DRAWING WAS CREATED IN MS PAINT IN 2008 BY AN ARTIST TRYING TO DRAW A CARTOON MOUSE.

1486 THE MOST LIKED PHOTO ON INSTAGRAM FOR A LONG TIME WAS JUST A PICTURE OF A REGULAR BROWN EGG, BEATING OUT WORLD-FAMOUS CELEBRITIES AND ATHLETES.

1487 THE "SUCCESS KID" MEME (A BABY CLENCHING HIS FIST IN VICTORY) HELPED RAISE ENOUGH MONEY ONLINE TO PAY FOR HIS DAD'S REAL-LIFE KIDNEY TRANSPLANT.

1488 MODERN DIGITAL ARTISTS USE DRAWING TABLETS WITH SPECIALIZED STYLUSES THAT CAN SENSE OVER 8,000 DIFFERENT LEVELS OF PRESSURE.

1489 AGATHA CHRISTIE IS THE BEST-SELLING FICTION WRITER OF ALL TIME, HAVING SOLD AN ESTIMATED 2 BILLION COPIES OF HER BOOKS.

1490 WILLIAM FAULKNER WROTE HIS FAMOUS NOVEL AS I LAY DYING IN JUST SIX WEEKS WHILE WORKING NIGHT SHIFTS AT A POWER PLANT, CLAIMING HE NEVER CHANGED A SINGLE WORD.

1491 THE CAPUCHIN MONKEY NAMED CRYSTAL, WHO STARRED IN NIGHT AT THE MUSEUM, HAS HER OWN IMDB PAGE AND HAS APPEARED IN OVER 20 MOVIES.

1492 SOCCER STAR LAMINE YAMAL STILL HAD TO BRING HIS HOMEWORK AND ATTEND ONLINE SCHOOL CLASSES WHILE HE WAS PLAYING IN MAJOR INTERNATIONAL TOURNAMENTS.

1493 IN THE CHINESE ZODIAC, THE RARE "FIRE HORSE" ONLY COMES AROUND ONCE EVERY 60 YEARS, WITH THE NEXT ONE HAPPENING IN 2026.

1494 THE SHAPE OF THE FAMOUS VIDEO GAME CHARACTER PAC-MAN WAS INSPIRED BY A PIZZA WITH A SINGLE SLICE MISSING.

1495 THE VOICE OF DARTH VADER (JAMES EARL JONES) AND THE MAN INSIDE THE SUIT (DAVID PROWSE) NEVER ACTUALLY MET DURING THE FILMING OF THE ORIGINAL STAR WARS.

1496 SPONGEBOB SQUAREPANTS CREATOR STEPHEN HILLENBURG WAS A REAL-LIFE MARINE BIOLOGY TEACHER BEFORE HE STARTED MAKING CARTOONS.

1497 THE ORIGINAL DESIGN FOR CHEWBACCA IN STAR WARS WAS INSPIRED BY GEORGE LUCAS'S GIANT, FLUFFY ALASKAN MALAMUTE DOG SITTING IN THE PASSENGER SEAT OF HIS CAR.

1498 DOCTOR WHO IS THE LONGEST-RUNNING SCI-FI TELEVISION SHOW IN HISTORY, STARTING ALL THE WAY BACK IN 1963.

1499 TOM KENNY, THE VOICE OF SPONGEBOB, ALSO VOICES THE NARRATOR OF THE POWERPUFF GIRLS AND THE ICE KING IN ADVENTURE TIME.

1500 IN THE PIXAR MOVIE INSIDE OUT, THE PIZZA TOPPING THAT DISGUSTS RILEY WAS CHANGED FROM BROCCOLI TO GREEN BELL PEPPERS FOR THE JAPANESE RELEASE, BECAUSE KIDS IN JAPAN ACTUALLY LIKE BROCCOLI.

1501 THE HEXAGONAL CARPET PATTERN IN THE OVERLOOK HOTEL IN THE MOVIE THE SHINING IS SO FAMOUS THAT PIXAR HID IT INSIDE SID'S HOUSE IN TOY STORY.

1502 IN ZOOTOPIA, THE NEWS ANCHORS CHANGE DEPENDING ON WHAT COUNTRY YOU WATCH THE MOVIE IN—A MOOSE IN CANADA, A CORGI IN THE UK, AND A KOALA IN AUSTRALIA.

1503 THE GUINNESS BOOK OF WORLD RECORDS WAS ORIGINALLY CREATED BY THE MANAGING DIRECTOR OF THE GUINNESS BREWERY SPECIFICALLY TO SETTLE ARGUMENTS TAKING PLACE IN PUBS.

1504 BEFORE CREATING SUPER MARIO, SHIGERU MIYAMOTO ORIGINALLY WANTED TO MAKE A POPEYE VIDEO GAME BUT COULDN'T GET THE RIGHTS.

1505 THE CLASSIC SUPER MARIO BROS. THEME SONG WAS THE VERY FIRST PIECE OF VIDEO GAME MUSIC TO BE PRESERVED IN THE US LIBRARY OF CONGRESS.

1506 THE SCREECHING SOUND OF THE TIE FIGHTERS IN STAR WARS WAS CREATED BY COMBINING AN ELEPHANT'S BELLOW WITH THE SOUND OF A CAR DRIVING ON WET PAVEMENT.

1507 THE FAMOUS HUM OF A STAR WARS LIGHTSABER WAS DISCOVERED BY ACCIDENT WHEN A MICROPHONE PASSED CLOSELY BY A BROKEN TELEVISION SET.

1508 J.K. ROWLING CHOSE THE NAME "HOGWARTS" FOR THE HARRY POTTER SCHOOL AFTER SEEING A HOGWORT PLANT DURING A VISIT TO THE KEW GARDENS IN NEW YORK.

1509 THE CREATOR OF THE POKÉMON FRANCHISE GOT THE IDEA FOR THE GAME FROM HIS CHILDHOOD HOBBY OF CATCHING AND COLLECTING INSECTS IN THE FOREST.

1510 THERE IS A REAL-LIFE HEAVY METAL BAND CALLED "HEVISAURUS" IN FINLAND THAT DRESSES UP IN GIANT DINOSAUR COSTUMES AND PLAYS KID-FRIENDLY METAL MUSIC.

1511 IN THE 2002 MOVIE SPIDER-MAN, TOBEY MAGUIRE ACTUALLY CAUGHT THE FOOD ON THE LUNCH TRAY IN A SINGLE TAKE WITHOUT ANY CGI, BUT IT TOOK HIM 156 TRIES TO GET IT RIGHT.

1512 THE FAMOUS "MOONWALK" DANCE WAS NOT INVENTED BY MICHAEL JACKSON; IT WAS BEING PERFORMED BY TAP DANCERS AND STREET PERFORMERS AS EARLY AS THE 1930S.

1513 THE ARTIST EDGAR DEGAS CREATED A FAMOUS SCULPTURE CALLED THE LITTLE DANCER, AND THE ORIGINAL VERSION HAD A TUTU MADE OF REAL FABRIC AND WORE REAL HUMAN HAIR.

1514 THE FAMOUS "ABBEY ROAD" ALBUM COVER BY THE BEATLES IS THE ONLY ONE OF THEIR ORIGINAL UK ALBUMS THAT DOES NOT FEATURE THE BAND'S NAME OR THE ALBUM TITLE ON THE FRONT.

1515 THE ORIGINAL TITLE OF THE MASSIVE HIT TV SHOW FRIENDS WAS GOING TO BE INSOMNIA CAFE.

1516 THE ACTOR WHO PLAYED THE ORIGINAL GODZILLA IN 1954 WORE A HEAVY RUBBER SUIT THAT WEIGHED 220 POUNDS AND WAS SO HOT HE COULD ONLY WEAR IT FOR THREE MINUTES AT A TIME.

1517 BOB ROSS FILMED HIS ENTIRE 11-YEAR RUN OF THE JOY OF PAINTING FOR FREE; HE MADE HIS MONEY SELLING ART SUPPLIES AND TEACHING CLASSES.

1518 IN THE CARTOON PHINEAS AND FERB, ALMOST EVERY SINGLE EPISODE FEATURES A SONG BECAUSE THE CREATORS PITCHED THE SHOW TO THE NETWORK WITH A GUITAR IN HAND.

1519 THE ICONIC POINTED "S" SHAPE THAT MILLIONS OF KIDS DRAW IN MIDDLE SCHOOL NOTEBOOKS HAS NO KNOWN ORIGIN AND IS JUST KNOWN ONLINE AS THE "UNIVERSAL S" OR "COOL S".

1520 THE ICONIC DESIGN OF THE GHOSTBUSTERS LOGO WAS CREATED BY THE FILM'S ASSOCIATE PRODUCER FOR FREE, AND IT IS NOW ONE OF THE MOST RECOGNIZED LOGOS IN THE WORLD.

1521 VINCENT VAN GOGH PAINTED HIS MASTERPIECE THE STARRY NIGHT PURELY FROM HIS IMAGINATION WHILE LOOKING OUT THE WINDOW OF A ROOM IN FRANCE.

1522 THE ORIGINAL VERSION OF THE MASSIVELY POPULAR VIDEO GAME MINECRAFT WAS CREATED IN JUST SIX DAYS BY A SINGLE DEVELOPER.

1523 THE CHARACTER OF BUGS BUNNY OFFICIALLY SERVED IN THE US MARINE CORPS DURING WWII AND WAS HONORABLY DISCHARGED AT THE END OF THE WAR AS A MASTER SERGEANT.

1524 THE CREATOR OF PETER PAN, J.M. BARRIE, GAVE ALL THE RIGHTS TO THE STORY TO A CHILDREN'S HOSPITAL IN LONDON SO THEY COULD ALWAYS COLLECT THE ROYALTIES TO HELP SICK KIDS.

1525 SHREK WAS ACTUALLY THE FIRST MOVIE TO EVER WIN THE ACADEMY AWARD FOR BEST ANIMATED FEATURE WHEN THE CATEGORY WAS NEWLY CREATED IN 2002.

1526 THE SCOOBY-DOO CHARACTERS WERE HEAVILY INSPIRED BY THE PERSONALITIES OF THE CAST FROM THE CLASSIC TV SHOW THE MANY LOVES OF DOBIE GILLIS.

1527 IN THE INCREDIBLES, THE ECCENTRIC FASHION DESIGNER EDNA MODE WAS VOICED BY THE FILM'S MALE DIRECTOR, BRAD BIRD.

1528 PEPPA PIG IS SO INCREDIBLY POPULAR WORLDWIDE THAT IT HAS CAUSED SOME AMERICAN CHILDREN TO START SPEAKING WITH BRITISH ACCENTS, A PHENOMENON DUBBED THE "PEPPA EFFECT".

1529 TAYLOR SWIFT'S THREE PET CATS, MEREDITH GREY, OLIVIA BENSON, AND BENJAMIN BUTTON, ARE ALL NAMED AFTER FAMOUS TELEVISION AND MOVIE CHARACTERS.

1530 THE ICONIC GREEN SLIME USED ON NICKELODEON GAME SHOWS WAS ORIGINALLY MADE OUT OF VANILLA PUDDING, APPLESAUCE, GREEN FOOD COLORING, AND OATMEAL.

1531 THE HUNGER GAMES AUTHOR SUZANNE COLLINS GOT THE IDEA FOR THE DYSTOPIAN BOOKS WHILE CHANNEL-SURFING BETWEEN REALITY TV SHOWS AND REAL NEWS FOOTAGE OF THE IRAQ WAR.

1532 IN FROZEN, THE ANIMATION TEAM BROUGHT A REAL, LIVE REINDEER INTO THE DISNEY STUDIO SO THEY COULD STUDY HOW IT MOVED AND ACCURATELY ANIMATE THE CHARACTER SVEN.

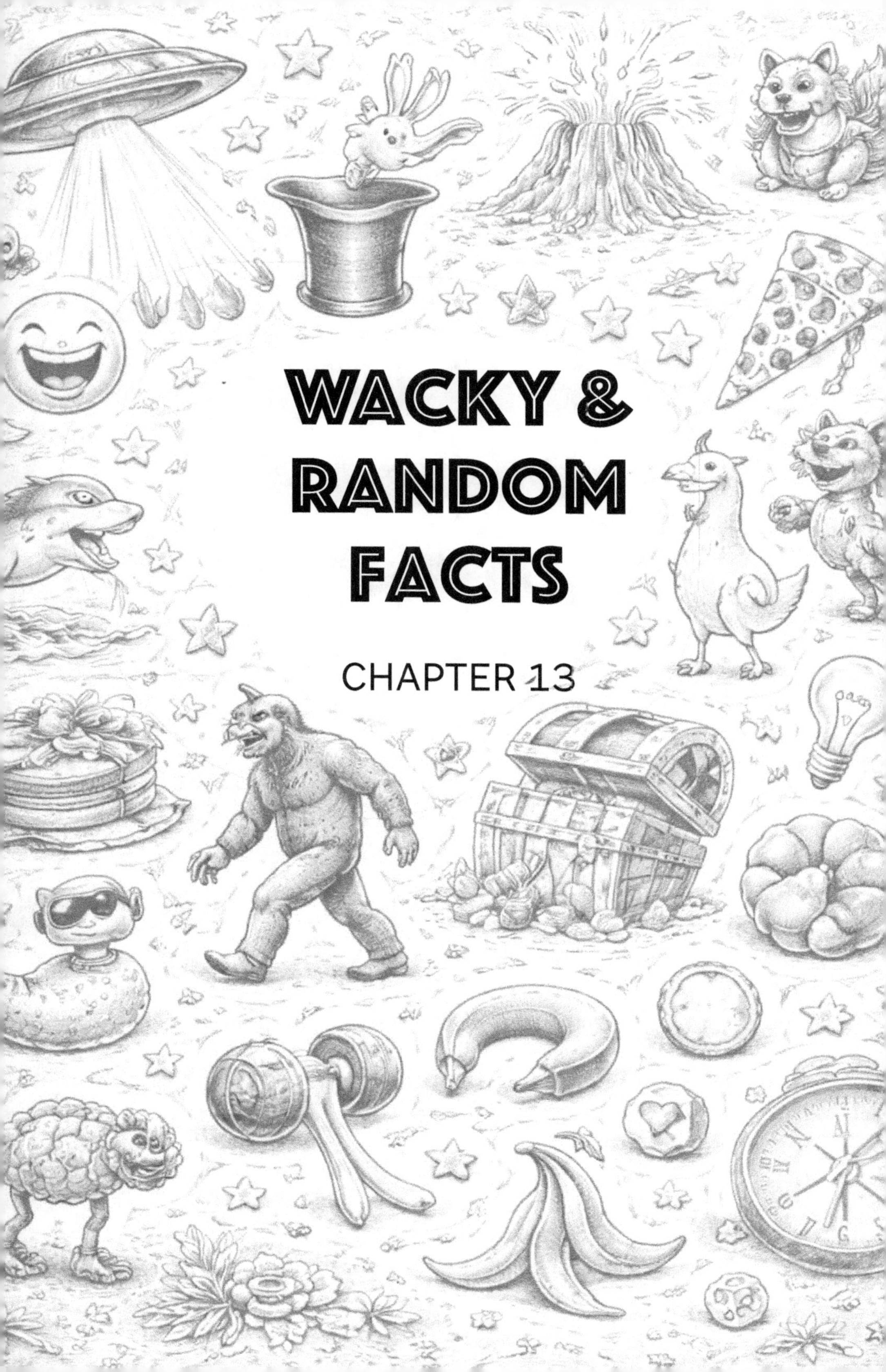

WACKY & RANDOM FACTS

CHAPTER 13

1533 THE EIFFEL TOWER CAN GROW MORE THAN SIX INCHES TALLER DURING THE SUMMER BECAUSE THE HEAT EXPANDS THE IRON.

1534 THE ELECTRIC CHAIR WAS INVENTED BY A DENTIST.

1535 PEOPLE IN CANADA EAT MORE MACARONI AND CHEESE THAN ANY OTHER NATION IN THE WORLD.

1536 FARMERS IN JAPAN GROW SQUARE WATERMELONS IN BOXES SO THEY ARE EASIER TO STACK.

1537 HIGH HEELS WERE ORIGINALLY DESIGNED FOR MEN TO HELP THEM RIDE HORSES.

1538 THE SHORTEST COMMERCIAL FLIGHT IN THE WORLD LASTS ONLY 57 SECONDS.

1539 AN ELEVEN-YEAR-OLD ACCIDENTALLY INVENTED THE POPSICLE BY LEAVING A SODA WITH A STIRRING STICK OUT IN THE COLD OVERNIGHT.

1540 BEFORE ERASERS WERE INVENTED, PEOPLE USED BREAD CRUMBS TO REMOVE PENCIL MARKS.

1541 THE AVERAGE PERSON WILL SPEND SIX MONTHS OF THEIR LIFE WAITING FOR RED LIGHTS TO TURN GREEN.

1542 BEFORE TOKYO, KYOTO WAS THE CAPITAL OF JAPAN. THE CITIES' NAMES ARE MADE UP OF THE SAME LETTERS.

1543 ZAMBIA AND ZIMBABWE ARE THE ONLY TWO COUNTRIES IN THE WORLD WITH NAMES BEGINNING WITH Z.

1544 A JIFFY IS A REAL UNIT OF TIME. IT IS THE TIME IT TAKES LIGHT TO TRAVEL ONE CENTIMETER IN A VACUUM.

1545 CELL PHONES USED TO BE THE SIZE OF BRICKS.

1546 ANCIENT GREEK THEATER AUDIENCES WOULD STAMP THEIR FEET RATHER THAN CLAP TO SHOW APPRECIATION.

1547 A 1 FOLLOWED BY 100 ZEROS IS A GOOGOL. A 1 FOLLOWED BY A GOOGOL OF ZEROS IS A GOOGOLPLEX.

1548 THE FLAG OF THE PHILIPPINES IS FLOWN UPSIDE DOWN WHEN THE COUNTRY IS AT WAR.

1549 THE POPE CANNOT BE AN ORGAN DONOR.

1550 THE BEARD OF A GOAT IS CALLED A GOATEE.

1551 MOST AMERICAN CAR HORNS HONK IN THE MUSICAL KEY OF F.

1552 THE UNITED STATES CENTRAL INTELLIGENCE AGENCY ONCE STRAPPED CAMERAS TO PIGEONS TRAINED TO FLY OVER ENEMY TARGETS.

1553 EARLY HOCKEY PUCKS WERE MADE FROM FROZEN COW DUNG.

1554 MORE THAN 200 PEOPLE COULD FIT IN THE WORLD'S BIGGEST IGLOO.

1555 HELIUM CAUSES YOUR VOICE TO SOUND HIGHER BECAUSE SOUND TRAVELS MORE QUICKLY THROUGH LIGHTER AIR.

1556 ARGENTINA'S PRESIDENT WORKS IN A BUILDING KNOWN AS LA CASA ROSADA (THE PINK HOUSE).

1557 SPIRAL STAIRCASES IN CASTLES OFTEN SPIRALED CLOCKWISE TO DISADVANTAGE RIGHT-HANDED ATTACKERS.

1558 ICELAND IS THE WORLD'S MOST PEACEFUL COUNTRY.

1559 THE METAL POTASSIUM EXPLODES WHEN IT TOUCHES WATER.

1560 COPPER IS A NATURAL BACTERIA KILLER, WHICH IS WHY MANY PUBLIC BUILDINGS HAVE COPPER DOOR HANDLES.

1561 THE METAL GALLIUM WILL MELT IN YOUR HANDS, BECAUSE IT TURNS FROM SOLID TO LIQUID AT 86°F (30°C).

1562 SWITZERLAND'S FLAG IS PERFECTLY SQUARE.

1563 THERE ARE NO LYRICS IN THE SPANISH NATIONAL ANTHEM.

1564 THE TIN CAN OPENER WAS INVENTED 48 YEARS AFTER THE TIN CAN ITSELF.

1565 A FIVE-MINUTE SHOWER USES 75 PERCENT LESS WATER THAN A BATH.

1566 IN GREECE, SHOWING YOUR PALM TO SOMEONE IS CONSIDERED OFFENSIVE.

1567 THERE IS NO ROMAN NUMERAL FOR THE NUMBER ZERO.

1568 CHINA AND INDIA MAKE UP MORE THAN A THIRD OF THE WORLD'S POPULATION.

1569 SOUTH AFRICA'S NATIONAL ANTHEM HAS FIVE VERSES, SUNG IN FIVE DIFFERENT LANGUAGES.

1570 THERE ARE MORE LAKES IN CANADA THAN IN ANY OTHER COUNTRY.

1571 THE STATUE OF LIBERTY'S OFFICIAL NAME IS LIBERTY ENLIGHTENING THE WORLD.

1572 THE MAN WHO INVENTED THE PRINGLES CAN WAS BURIED INSIDE ONE.

1573 THE STATE OF FLORIDA IS BIGGER THAN THE ENTIRE COUNTRY OF ENGLAND.

1574 THE LONGEST WEDDING VEIL EVER WORN WAS THE SAME LENGTH AS 63 FOOTBALL FIELDS.

1575 A SINGLE PIECE OF CONFETTI IS CALLED A CONFETTO.

1576 THE LONGEST HICCUPING SPREE IN HISTORY LASTED 68 YEARS.

1577 A VIOLIN CONTAINS ABOUT 70 SEPARATE PIECES OF WOOD.

1578 RUBBER BANDS LAST LONGER WHEN THEY ARE KEPT IN THE REFRIGERATOR.

1579 BEFORE ALARM CLOCKS WERE INVENTED, PEOPLE CALLED "KNOCKER-UPS" WERE HIRED TO TAP ON WINDOWS WITH LONG STICKS TO WAKE PEOPLE UP.

1580 THERE ARE MORE PLASTIC FLAMINGOS IN THE UNITED STATES THAN REAL ONES.

1581 THE INFINITY SIGN IS TECHNICALLY CALLED A LEMNISCATE.

1582 THE AVERAGE PERSON SPENDS TWO WEEKS OF THEIR LIFE WAITING FOR TRAFFIC LIGHTS TO CHANGE.

1583 THE HOLLYWOOD SIGN IN LOS ANGELES ORIGINALLY SAID "HOLLYWOODLAND".

1584 THE EIFFEL TOWER HAS 1,665 STEPS.

1585 MORE PEOPLE ARE BITTEN BY OTHER PEOPLE IN NEW YORK CITY EVERY YEAR THAN BY SHARKS WORLDWIDE.

1586 THE ISLANDS OF HAWAII MOVE ABOUT FOUR INCHES CLOSER TO JAPAN EVERY YEAR.

1587 THE AMAZON RIVER FLOWS FOR THOUSANDS OF MILES BUT HAS ZERO BRIDGES CROSSING IT.

1588 THE COUNTRY OF SUDAN HAS MORE PYRAMIDS THAN EGYPT.

1589 RUSSIA IS SO BIG THAT IT COVERS 11 DIFFERENT TIME ZONES.

1590 MAINE IS THE CLOSEST U.S. STATE TO THE CONTINENT OF AFRICA.

1591 THE MONA LISA HAS NO EYEBROWS.

1592 A CON MAN ONCE SUCCESSFULLY SOLD THE EIFFEL TOWER FOR SCRAP METAL.

1593 THE STATUE OF LIBERTY IS GREEN BECAUSE THE COPPER SKIN HAS OXIDIZED OVER TIME.

1594 FRANCE COVERS MORE TIME ZONES THAN ANY OTHER COUNTRY BECAUSE OF ITS OVERSEAS TERRITORIES.

1595 ISTANBUL, TURKEY, IS THE ONLY CITY IN THE WORLD LOCATED ON TWO CONTINENTS.

1596 VATICAN CITY IS THE SMALLEST COUNTRY IN THE WORLD; IT FITS INSIDE THE CITY OF ROME.

1597 FIRE DOES NOT CAST A SHADOW BECAUSE A FLAME IS A SOURCE OF LIGHT ITSELF.

1598 HOT WATER CAN SOMETIMES FREEZE FASTER THAN COLD WATER; THIS IS CALLED THE MPEMBA EFFECT.

1599 A SINGLE PENCIL HAS ENOUGH GRAPHITE TO WRITE ABOUT 45,000 WORDS.

1600 THE FIRST PERSON TO BE ARRESTED FOR SPEEDING WAS DRIVING A CAR AT 8 MILES PER HOUR.

1601 THE PLASTIC TIP AT THE END OF A SHOELACE IS CALLED AN AGLET.

1602 A "MOMENT" WAS AN ACTUAL UNIT OF TIME IN MEDIEVAL ENGLAND, EQUAL TO 90 SECONDS.

1603 A U.S. QUARTER HAS EXACTLY 119 RIDGES ON ITS EDGE, WHILE A DIME HAS 118.

1604 THERE ARE 293 DIFFERENT WAYS TO MAKE CHANGE FOR A U.S. DOLLAR BILL.

1605 MOST LIPSTICK CONTAINS FISH SCALES TO GIVE IT THAT SHIMMERY LOOK.

1606 REAL PEARLS WILL MELT IF THEY ARE PLACED IN A BOWL OF VINEGAR.

1607 ALASKA IS TECHNICALLY THE MOST EASTERN AND WESTERN STATE IN THE U.S. BECAUSE ITS ISLANDS CROSS THE 180TH MERIDIAN.

1608 THE WHITE DASHED LINES ON A HIGHWAY ARE ACTUALLY 10 FEET LONG, EVEN THOUGH THEY LOOK SHORT WHEN YOU DRIVE PAST THEM.

1609 THERE IS A TOWN IN NORWAY CALLED "HELL" THAT FREEZES OVER EVERY WINTER.

1610 THE LITTLE PLASTIC TABLE IN THE MIDDLE OF A PIZZA BOX IS OFFICIALLY CALLED A "PIZZA SAVER".

1611 THE TINY POCKET INSIDE THE FRONT POCKET OF YOUR JEANS WAS ORIGINALLY DESIGNED TO HOLD A POCKET WATCH.

1612 JAPAN HAS A NETWORK OF "MELODY ROADS" WITH GROOVES CUT INTO THE ASPHALT THAT PLAY MUSIC WHEN YOU DRIVE OVER THEM AT THE RIGHT SPEED.

1613 THE EIFFEL TOWER WAS ORIGINALLY INTENDED TO BE A TEMPORARY STRUCTURE FOR A FAIR.

1614 THE STATUE OF LIBERTY WEARS A SIZE 879 SHOE.

1615 THE EMPIRE STATE BUILDING HAS ITS OWN ZIP CODE.

1616 BEFORE "CHEESE," PEOPLE SAID "PRUNES" WHEN TAKING PHOTOS TO KEEP THEIR MOUTHS SMALL.

1617 RENO, NEVADA IS FARTHER WEST THAN LOS ANGELES, CALIFORNIA.

1618 NAURU IS THE ONLY COUNTRY IN THE WORLD WITH NO OFFICIAL CAPITAL CITY.

1619 90% OF THE WORLD'S POPULATION LIVES IN THE NORTHERN HEMISPHERE.

1620 A CHEF'S HAT HAS 100 PLEATS TO REPRESENT THE 100 WAYS TO COOK AN EGG.

1621 IT IS ILLEGAL TO CHEW GUM IN SINGAPORE (WITH A FEW EXCEPTIONS).

1622 WATER IS ONE OF THE FEW SUBSTANCES THAT EXPANDS WHEN IT FREEZES, WHICH IS WHY ICE CUBES TAKE UP MORE SPACE THAN WATER.

1623 PUMICE IS THE ONLY ROCK IN THE WORLD THAT FLOATS IN WATER.

1624 CANADA HAS A "POLAR BEAR JAIL" FOR BEARS THAT WANDER INTO THE TOWN OF CHURCHILL.

1625 THE DEEPEST POSTBOX IN THE WORLD IS 10 METERS UNDERWATER IN JAPAN.

1626 THE PLASTIC THING THAT LETS YOU ADJUST A BACKPACK STRAP IS CALLED A "LADDER LOCK".

1627 THE METAL BAND THAT HOLDS A PENCIL ERASER IN PLACE IS CALLED A FERRULE.

1628 A BILLION SECONDS IS ABOUT 32 YEARS.

1629 A "SHAKE" IS A REAL UNIT OF TIME EQUAL TO 10 NANOSECONDS.

1630 THE LEANING TOWER OF PISA IS HOLLOW ON THE INSIDE.

1631 BETTY WHITE WAS BORN BEFORE SLICED BREAD WAS INVENTED.

1632 THE HANDSHAKE WAS ORIGINALLY CREATED TO PROVE YOU WEREN'T HOLDING A WEAPON.

1633 MORE MONOPOLY MONEY IS PRINTED EVERY YEAR THAN REAL U.S. CURRENCY.

1634 THE LITTLE LOOP ON THE BACK OF A DRESS SHIRT IS CALLED A "LOCKER LOOP".

1635 IN AN EMERGENCY, A CRAYON CAN BURN LIKE A CANDLE FOR ABOUT 30 MINUTES.

1636 THE WORLD'S SMALLEST PARK IS LOCATED IN PORTLAND, OREGON, AND IS ONLY TWO FEET WIDE.

1637 THE INDENTATION AT THE BOTTOM OF A WINE BOTTLE IS OFFICIALLY CALLED A "PUNT".

1638 A CAT NAMED STUBBS WAS THE HONORARY MAYOR OF A TOWN IN ALASKA FOR 20 YEARS.

1639 PIRATES WORE EARRINGS BECAUSE THEY BELIEVED THE PRESSURE POINTS IN THE EARLOBE IMPROVED THEIR EYESIGHT.

1640 THE EMPIRE STATE BUILDING GETS STRUCK BY LIGHTNING ABOUT 25 TIMES A YEAR.

1641 NEON SIGNS CAN ONLY BE RED; OTHER COLORS ARE MADE BY USING DIFFERENT GASES LIKE ARGON OR KRYPTON.

1642 PAPER MONEY IN THE UNITED STATES IS NOT PAPER; IT IS A BLEND OF 75% COTTON AND 25% LINEN.

1643 THE PENTAGON HAS TWICE AS MANY BATHROOMS AS NECESSARY BECAUSE IT WAS BUILT WHEN LAWS REQUIRED SEPARATE FACILITIES.

1644 ANTARCTICA HAS A FLAG, BUT IT HAS NO OFFICIAL COUNTRY OR GOVERNMENT.

1645 THE "SPOT" ON A 7UP BOTTLE COMES FROM ITS INVENTOR, WHO HAD RED EYES.

1646 MR. ROGERS' MOM KNITTED ALL THE SWEATERS HE WORE ON HIS SHOW.

1647 GODZILLA HAS BEEN GRANTED OFFICIAL CITIZENSHIP IN JAPAN.

1648 A "BUTT" IS A REAL MEDIEVAL UNIT OF MEASUREMENT FOR WINE, EQUAL TO 126 GALLONS.

1649 THERE IS A TOWN IN OREGON CALLED BORING, AND IT IS SISTER CITIES WITH A TOWN IN SCOTLAND CALLED DULL.

1650 THE FIRST PASSENGERS ON A HOT AIR BALLOON WERE A SHEEP, A DUCK, AND A ROOSTER.

1651 THERE IS A TOWN IN ALASKA NAMED "CHICKEN" BECAUSE THE FOUNDERS COULDN'T AGREE ON HOW TO SPELL "PTARMIGAN" (A TYPE OF BIRD).

1652 THE CARDBOARD SLEEVE ON A COFFEE CUP HAS AN OFFICIAL NAME: A ZARF.

1653 THE TINY METAL BALL INSIDE A CAN OF SPRAY PAINT IS CALLED A "PEA".

1654 THE WIRE CAGE THAT HOLDS A CHAMPAGNE CORK IN PLACE IS CALLED A MUSELET.

1655 THE PRONGS ON A FORK ARE OFFICIALLY CALLED TINES.

1656 THE SIDE OF A HAMMER IS CALLED A CHEEK.

1657 THE LITTLE LOOPS ON YOUR JEANS THAT HOLD YOUR BELT ARE CALLED "KEEPERS".

1658 THE FLAPS ON A JUICE BOX ARE OFFICIALLY CALLED "EARS".

1659 THE DIAMOND-SHAPED LEATHER PATCH ON A BACKPACK IS CALLED A "LASH TAB" AND IS USED FOR TYING GEAR TO YOUR BAG.

1660 NONE OF THE BEATLES COULD READ OR WRITE SHEET MUSIC.

1661 VINCENT VAN GOGH ONLY SOLD ONE PAINTING WHILE HE WAS ALIVE.

1662 THE TOWN OF SAINT-LOUIS-DU-HA! HA! IN CANADA IS THE ONLY TOWN NAME IN THE WORLD WITH TWO EXCLAMATION POINTS.

1663 PRESIDENT WILLIAM HOWARD TAFT WAS SO LARGE THAT HE ONCE GOT STUCK IN THE WHITE HOUSE BATHTUB AND HAD TO BE PULLED OUT BY SIX MEN.

1664 FRUIT STICKERS ARE EDIBLE, AND THE GLUE USED TO ATTACH THEM IS FOOD-GRADE.

1665 CHEESE IS THE MOST STOLEN FOOD ITEM IN THE WORLD.

1666 CANADA HAS A DESIGNATED UFO LANDING PAD IN THE TOWN OF ST. PAUL, ALBERTA.

1667 LIECHTENSTEIN IS SO SMALL THAT YOU CAN RENT THE ENTIRE COUNTRY FOR A NIGHT.

1668 A "MICRO-CENTURY" IS A REAL UNIT OF TIME EQUAL TO ABOUT 52 MINUTES.

1669 TREES CAN ACTUALLY EXPLODE IF IT GETS COLD ENOUGH, BECAUSE THE SAP FREEZES AND EXPANDS.

1670 NEPAL IS THE ONLY COUNTRY IN THE WORLD WHOSE FLAG IS NOT A SQUARE OR A RECTANGLE; IT IS TWO STACKED TRIANGLES.

1671 THE COUNTRY OF BHUTAN MEASURES "GROSS NATIONAL HAPPINESS" INSTEAD OF ECONOMIC GROWTH.

1672 THE PATENT FOR THE FIRE HYDRANT WAS LOST IN A FIRE AT THE PATENT OFFICE.

1673 THE SYMBOL FOR THE "POWER" BUTTON IS A COMBINATION OF THE NUMBERS 0 AND 1 (REPRESENTING OFF AND ON).

1674 BENJAMIN FRANKLIN INVENTED SWIM FINS WHEN HE WAS JUST 11 YEARS OLD.

1675 THOMAS EDISON HAD A TATTOO OF FIVE DOTS ON HIS ARM.

1676 THE U.S. GOVERNMENT HAS A WRITTEN TRAINING PLAN FOR A "ZOMBIE APOCALYPSE" CALLED CONPLAN 8888.

1677 AFRICA IS THE ONLY CONTINENT THAT TOUCHES ALL FOUR HEMISPHERES (NORTH, SOUTH, EAST, AND WEST).

1678 THE "ZONE OF SILENCE" IN MEXICO IS A DESERT AREA WHERE RADIO SIGNALS STRANGELY FAIL TO WORK.

1679 THERE ARE MORE PUBLIC LIBRARIES IN THE UNITED STATES THAN THERE ARE MCDONALD'S RESTAURANTS.

1680 IN 2006, AN AUSTRALIAN MAN JOKINGLY TRIED TO SELL THE ENTIRE COUNTRY OF NEW ZEALAND ON EBAY.

1681 THE WORLD'S LARGEST RUBBER DUCK IS 59 FEET TALL AND WEIGHS OVER 1,000 POUNDS.

1682 THE GUINNESS WORLD RECORD FOR THE LOUDEST BURP IS 112.7 DECIBELS, WHICH IS LOUDER THAN A MOTORCYCLE.

1683 THE LARGEST PUMPKIN EVER GROWN WEIGHED MORE THAN A SMALL CAR (OVER 2,700 POUNDS).

1684 THE SHORTEST SONG EVER COMMERCIALLY RECORDED IS "YOU SUFFER" BY A BAND CALLED NAPALM DEATH, LASTING EXACTLY 1.316 SECONDS.

1685 THE WORLD'S LARGEST GRAND PIANO WAS BUILT BY A 15-YEAR-OLD AND IS OVER 18 FEET LONG.

1686 SLIME MOLDS DON'T HAVE BRAINS, BUT THEY ARE SMART ENOUGH TO SUCCESSFULLY NAVIGATE AND SOLVE MAZES TO FIND FOOD.

1687 THE TOTAL WEIGHT OF ALL THE EARTH'S ATMOSPHERE IS ABOUT 5.5 QUADRILLION TONS.

1688 A TOWN IN HONDURAS EXPERIENCES A PHENOMENON WHERE IT "RAINS FISH" FROM THE SKY ONCE A YEAR.

1689 THE WORLD RECORD FOR THE MOST T-SHIRTS WORN AT ONCE IS 257.

1690 THERE IS AN ANNUAL WORLD TOE WRESTLING CHAMPIONSHIP HELD IN THE UK.

1691 THE LONGEST TIME BETWEEN TWO TWINS BEING BORN IS 87 DAYS.

1692 THE FIRST ROLLER COASTER IN AMERICA WAS OPENED IN 1884 AT CONEY ISLAND.

1693 A MAN ONCE SET A RECORD BY BALANCING A 350-POUND MINI COOPER CAR ON HIS HEAD.

1694 A SINGLE STRAND OF SPIDER SILK STRETCHING AROUND THE EARTH WOULD WEIGH ONLY ABOUT ONE POUND.

1695 THE NATIONAL ANIMAL OF SCOTLAND IS THE UNICORN.

1696 THERE ARE MORE TREES ON EARTH THAN THERE ARE STARS IN THE MILKY WAY GALAXY.

1697 THE WORD "GORILLA" TRANSLATES TO "A TRIBE OF HAIRY WOMEN."

1698 A GROUP OF PUGS IS OFFICIALLY CALLED A "GRUMBLE."

1699 THE BLOB OF TOOTHPASTE ON YOUR BRUSH HAS AN OFFICIAL NAME: "NURDLE."

www.ingramcontent.com/pod-product-compliance
Lightning Source LLC
Chambersburg PA
CBHW051050050726
47592CB00002B/472

* 9 7 8 1 9 4 8 6 5 2 8 5 8 *